OVER $5,000,000,000,000 CLAIMED!

SO SUE ME!

by

JOE KOHUT

BLACK TOOTH PRESS
PHILADELPHIA, PA

So Sue Me
© 1993 by Joe Kohut

Library of Congress Catalog Number: 93-72204
ISBN: 0-9628362-2-2

Printed in the United States of America

First edition September 1993

Black Tooth Press
768 North 26th St.
Philadelphia, PA 19130
215-232-6611

For my brother, John, for his generous heart, and for constantly reminding me that if you have a strong enough stomach, human beings are an infinite source of enjoyment.

Acknowledgements

I would like to recognize the contributions of a number of people, without whom this project would not have seen the light of day. Jim and Lisa Anderson, for calling the right hander out of the bullpen; Charles Carr, Gary Schaffer and Jennifer Shropshier for making the necessary hardware, software and intellectual Tupperware available; Don and Hether Smith and their friend Mr. Weller for keeping the emotional ship of state afloat; Louis Gribaudo for providing critical feedback; Carrie Marston for doing dirty work without even one dirty look; Ronnie Polaneczky and Doug Candeaub for helping keep things kosher; and, as always, all my love and thanks to Janet.

Introduction

On a spring day in 1983, sitting in the shotgun seat of a VW Beetle, I headed out of East Los Angeles for Bugsy Siegel's great American theme park, Las Vegas. The driver, a retired gangster turned computer maven, was also my next door neighbor. "The Count," as he was known, had just scored a coup in copper futures, and we were off to test his mathematically foolproof system for turning grubstake into bonanza at the craps table. Unfortunately for him, he had only perfected the first part of the system and after doubling his money on the first pass, The Count went and lost every penny. We spent the rest of the night in the keno parlor of the MGM Grand, trying to win enough money for a room at the inn.

It was while we were in the keno parlor that The Count told me how he landed in copper in the first place. Even though he had a Turkish surname (courtesy of a sailor that swam into the gene pool several generations back), The Count was as Chicano as homemade menudo. And he had learned, over time, that his ethnicity held a particular value in the marketplace. His investment in copper was financed by money won in his most recent discrimination suit against a former employer. It seems that he had developed a facility for getting hired to work in the computer departments of major corporations. Then, when he was convinced that he had encountered discrimination in the work place, based on his color or his name, he would sue his employer for a tidy sum. (And Count, if you're still out there, I'm sure that they were all righteous beefs.) When last I heard, he was batting a solid three for three.

Clearly, The Count was a man ahead of his time. Even as recently as ten years ago, the notion of lawsuit as cottage industry was still fairly uncommon. Little did we know that it was gaining acceptance as everyone's chance at the brass ring, and was headed in our collective direction like a tornado toward a trailer park.

So we offer for your consideration, as Mr. Serling used to say, over 300 examples of individuals and institutions who tried to get either satisfaction or their piece of the pie by going to court. Some of the stories we chose because we were dismayed that the plaintiff actually thought that taking legal action was a good idea. In others, it was the behavior of the defendant that made us shake our collective head. In still others, it was the finding of the jury that left us dumbstruck.

All of the material that follows was collected from the public record, the majority of the stories coming from local newspapers and legal publications. In all cases, individuals have been named in the stories as they were named in the original material. We have included criminal cases because they are of a type of lawsuit brought on behalf of the public good (and the stories were too good to pass up). Motions, appeals and second thoughts being what they are, it is possible that many of these cases have moved on to more fertile legal pastures since this book went to press. If you have an update on any of the lawsuits that follow, or a favorite lawsuit that doesn't appear here, we would love to hear about it. Just send a copy of the story as it originally appeared, including source and date, to your friends at Black Tooth Press.

"I'm gonna go get a drink."

According to Marydawna Davis, the ad was very clear. International House of Pancakes, IHOP to the initiated, was offering the "Sweet 16" breakfast special for $2.49. It included two pancakes, two eggs, sausage and bacon. Imagine her disappointment when the IHOP in Concord, California told her that it wasn't serving the "Sweet 16." In addition to disappointment, Davis claimed in her $2 billion suit that she experienced "a burning in the stomach from hunger, emotional distress and humiliation, hurt feelings..." You get the picture.

So did IHOP, who offered to settle with Davis out of court. Two free meals? Nope. $1,000? Nope again. "This just insulted me further," said Davis, who just happens to be an attorney. After all, she had experienced $2 billion worth of hurt feelings. The suit was dismissed, but Davis planned to appeal. Probably after a good breakfast.

A former student (or should that be students?) sued the University of Illinois after it dismissed him for plagiarizing a school assignment. Larry Sanders, a graduate student in speech and hearing sciences, claimed that he has multiple personalities, and one of those other Larrys, not the good Larry, submitted the plagiarized document. Sanders also wanted it understood that this was done without the knowledge or approval of the rest of the Larrys.

The suit requested his reinstatement as a student.

⚖

The Kansas Supreme Court ruled that Shane Seyer was obligated to pay child support to Colleen Hermesmann for her daughter, the issue of an illicit affair that took place when Seyer was 13 and Hermesmann was 17. She was his baby sitter at the time.

Seyer claimed that he shouldn't have to pay support since he was legally unable to consent to sex at the time he impregnated Hermesmann.

⚖

Anne Marie Lindsay, a topless dancer in Dallas, just wouldn't take no for an answer. Claiming that she was denied a job because of her age, Ms. Lindsay took the matter to court, and appealed when the first judge dismissed her case.

Fortunately for her, chivalry is alive and well in

the 5th U.S. District Court, which ruled that the first judge should not have dismissed her discrimination claim just because he didn't think she had the looks for the job.

⚖️

Tommy Lynn Lewis, an inmate at the Clark County Jail in Vancouver, Washington, tried to put the jail's cuisine into a constitutional context. The jail had been serving "nutra-loaf" to inmates who have a history of throwing food or are "assaultive and volatile." An all-in-one meal, the loaf consisted of vegetables, meat, oatmeal and crackers. It was baked in 12½ pound logs and served in an 8oz. portion which the jail claimed to be a complete meal.

Lewis claimed that eating the "nutra-loaf" had caused him mental and physical distress and asked the court for punitive damages. One can only assume that Tommy Lynn isn't too crazy about scrapple either.

⚖️

Max Baer, Jr., the man who we all came to know and love as Jethro on the Beverly Hillbillies, has gone on to become a Hollywood producer. That means he gets to sue people. Which he did, claiming that ABC-TV interfered with his plan to turn Madonna's hit song "Like a Virgin" into a feature film.

A court agreed with Baer and awarded him $2 million in damages. The mind boggles at the thought of the project that might have been.

Some folks don't know when to quit. Attorney Bruce R. Atkins sued Farmers Mutual Fire Insurance Co., claiming that they owe him $2.05 million in damages because of a fire that levelled a house he was renovating. At the time of the trial, he revised his claim to a more modest $42,000. It wasn't quite modest enough.

A six-member jury in New Jersey ruled that the fire was set by Atkins or someone acting at his direction and threw the claim out of court. Atkins, whose license to practice law is under suspension for an unrelated matter, said upon leaving the courtroom that nothing criminal had taken place. The county prosecutor isn't quite so certain, and is reviewing the case.

⚖

Convicted killer William McKiney is probably not a strict constructionist when it comes to constitutional matters. He claimed that environmental tobacco smoke, also known as secondary smoke, threatened his health and therefore violates the constitutional prohibition against our old friends "cruel and unusual punishment." So, naturally, McKiney sued the Nevada state prison system, his current place of residence, seeking monetary damages and a smoke-free environment.

Thirty-three states have joined Nevada's challenge to the appeal. Hawaii attorney General Warren Price III argued that a ban on smoking in prison might make prisoners more prone to violence and speculated on an administrative nightmare caused by attempting to segregate inmates based on smoking status. (Good evening, Mr. Serial Killer, will that be smoking or non-smoking?) McKiney's case will be heard by the U.S. Supreme Court.

⚖

Andrea Pizzo said that the University of Maine had a Jersey heifer with a dangerous disposition and a personality problem that should have been evident to the folks in the Livestock Management Deptartment. Pizzo sued the school for failing to protect her from the battering bovine and for damages to her wrist and knee, suffered when the 400-pound heifer knocked her against the wall of its pen.

No word yet on whether the court thought her suit was udderly without merit.

⚖

In a contemporary version of "the devil made me do it," Leonard Tose, former owner of the Philadelphia Eagles professional football team, claimed in a lawsuit that he shouldn't be held responsible for losing $199,000 over four days of gambling at the Sands Hotel and Casino in Atlantic City. Tose said he was so visibly intoxicated, and kept that way intentionally by the Sands' endless rounds of Dewar's and Perrier, that the casino should not have allowed him to gamble. Court documents indicate that Tose lost $14.6 million gambling in Atlantic City casinos between 1981 and 1986.

A nine-member jury rejected the first part of Tose's claim involving the $199,000, as did the 4th U.S. District Court on appeal. Upon leaving the courthouse, Tose commented, "I'm gonna go get a drink."

⚖

Coconut oil is not natural. At least not according to those folks at Kellogg, who filed a $100 million lawsuit against our old friends at General Mills, claiming that they engaged in misleading advertising when they called Post Natural Raisin Bran "natural." The breakfast cereal is coated with coconut oil.

Kellogg also claimed that Post's Raisin Bran was less than natural because "extraneous material that would [normally] cling to the raisins had been cleaned off." That's probably not a big disappointment for most folks.

⚖

Michael Vaughn sued the Shrine Temple in Lexington, Kentucky for punitive damages and intentional infliction of emotional distress, claiming he was injured during the fraternity's secret initiation rights. Vaughn claimed that he was stripped to his boxer shorts, threatened with a branding iron and received electrical shock to his buttocks, which were then sprayed with red paint. He claimed he was then shocked twice more before sliding off a table which had been surrounded with vats of strawberries, ice cream and whipped cream. Vaughn hit his head on the floor and was knocked out. You can see why he wanted to join in the first place.

In court, the Shriners conceded that shocks are sometimes administered to initiates but that the experience is supposed to startle, not hurt them. They also said that members sometimes test the devices on themselves. "The way he tells it, it sounds a lot worse than it actually is," said temple attorney Greg Jenkins.

⚖

San Diego attorney Myron Klarfeld was flagged by security guards at a federal courthouse when he tried to pass through the metal detector. It seems that the alarm was set off by the metal shank in his loafers.

The guards made it clear to Klarfeld that in order to enter the courthouse he would have to remove his shoes. Against his wishes, Klarfeld complied, walking "several yards in his stocking feet, much to the amusement of the guard and onlookers." Knowing a constitutional issue when he smells one, Klarfeld challenged the policy in court, calling it an unreasonable search and thus a violation of the Fourth Amendment.

⚖

Edward Espinosa was seven years old when he accidentally knocked a piping-hot plate of mashed potatoes and gravy into his lap. This, however, was not your average case of spilled spuds. Edward was fooling around in the Heaton Elementary School cafeteria during that fateful lunch hour, and as sure as one man's active kid is another man's case of negligence, Edward's dad sued the Fresno Unified School District. Mr. Espinosa claimed that the district was negligent in its supervision of the lunch room and as a result of that negligence, his son had been burned.

"To me, it's the same as if a school bus driver runs a stop sign," said Espinosa's attorney. The school district's lawyer argued that California law required all hot food to be served at a temperature of 140° F. Food consultant Julie Chernoff doubted that the evidence in the case could stand up in a jury trial. "When was the last time you got anything remotely hot from a school cafeteria?" she asked.

⚖

Gillette's advertising folks created a commercial that demonstrated that Tame Creme Rinse was easier to rinse off of a pane of glass than Alberto-Culver's Balsam Creme Rinse. Alberto-Culver begged to differ, and responded with a $7 million lawsuit.

No indication yet as to why anyone would want to spread creme rinse on a pane of glass in the first place.

⚖

The Joint Free Library of Morristown and Morris Township, New Jersey had had enough of Richard Kreimer. Kreimer had been asked to leave the library several times because he was considered a nuisance and was allegedly a disruptive presence:

14

staring at employees and patrons, following them around and emitting a stench so foul that no one would sit near him.

Kreimer sued the library, preparing the filing himself. He claimed that the library's newly-instituted "patron policy" discriminated against the homeless. Kreimer also filed another suit against the local police and township officials, complaining of harassment. Proving that not everyone who smells bad is nuts, Kreimer won his suit against the library while the police and town settled out of court, producing a six-figure windfall for himself.

⚖

According to one inmate at the Dixon Correctional Center, clothes don't make the man or the religion. The 48-year-old murderer claimed to be a member in good standing of the Technicians of the Sacred, a religion based on "magical systems" and nudity.

He contended, in a federal lawsuit, that by making him wear clothes to the prison chapel, the Illinois facility was violating his First Amendment rights.

⚖

On November 2, 1991, Chicago attorney Frank D. Zaffere III proposed to Maria Dillon, closing the deal by giving Ms. Dillon a 1.06 carat diamond ring. By the following June, however, Ms. Dillon was having second thoughts and broke off the engagement. When he got the news, her former fiance didn't simply ask for his ring back. You guessed it, Zaffere sued for breach of contract.

Zaffere figured that during the course of the relationship he had spent $40,310.48 on Ms. Dillon and that's what he wanted, to the penny. You have to wonder which is stranger -- that Zaffere sued her in the first place, or that he was able to do it in accordance with the provisions of something called the Illinois Breach of Promise Act. And doubly odd that no one has ever tried to apply that law to the Chicago Cubs.

⚖️

Jack Sherman, guitarist for the Red Hot Chili Peppers from 1983 to 1985, hit his former bandmates with a breach-of-contract suit for an unspecified amount, claiming damages and back royalties. He also claims that he was abused both physically and verbally by lead singer Anthony Kiedis and the Chili's ever-popular bass player, Flea.

When asked why he waited so long to register a complaint, his attorney said , "Sometimes you don't know you've been damaged until later." Or, he might have added, until someone has a hit record.

⚖️

When Iona Klein arrived at Mr. G's convenience store on the morning of April 7, 1992, she found a lottery ticket that had been ordered by a customer but never actually purchased. According to Klein, an employee of Mr. G's, she purchased and kept the ticket.

16

The ticket was the winner in the April 6 Lotto America drawing and was worth $12.5 million.

As you might suspect, store owners Mike and Diane Dacy thought that they had a prior claim to the ticket and went to court to prevent Iona from cashing the ticket. Robin Parsons, the clerk who issued the winning ticket, also entered a claim against Klein, arguing that since she would have had to pay for the ticket if it went unsold, she also had ownership rights. Apparently unfazed by the controversy, Klein entered the court proceedings wearing a T-shirt that read, "Finders Keepers, Losers Weepers."

⚖

Fifteen-year-old Matthew Lucas claims that his mother has refused to see him since he left in 1991 to live with his father. In what attorneys say is a new application of the British Children's Act, Matthew has asked the court to intervene and force his mother to see him.

Lucas says that despite what she has done, he will always love his mother. There is no indication yet of his mom mounting a countersuit.

⚖

In October of 1991, a German couple set sail on the *Pearl of the Caribbean* for what they thought would be a peaceful and relaxing two-week Caribbean cruise. They later told a Frankfurt court that they didn't realize at the time that they would be accompanied on their journey by the Swiss Union of Friends of Folk Music. Swiss yodelers. Five hundred of them. And that doesn't count the brass band that serenaded the guests at the intimate midnight buffet.

The Frankfurt court ordered the shipping company to refund one-third of the $4,478 that the couple had paid for their adventure. You can't blame them for suing -- after all, the yodeling artistry of the Village Sparrows of Oberaegeri probably starts to wear thin after a while.

⚖

In 1991, a federal judge in Seattle ruled that Kimberly Clark, the maker of Huggies, was the first to invent a design feature that reduced leaks in its diapers. However, the judge also ruled that Procter & Gamble, makers of both Pampers and Luvs diapers did not infringe on Kimberly-Clark's patent when they introduced their own anti-leak feature.

This followed legal rulings on patent disputes between the two diaper giants in 1989, 1987 and 1985. You can see how hard it has been to get to the bottom of things.

⚖

As we all know, throwing horseshoes and hand grenades used to be the only games in which being close counted. Well, the Ohio Supreme Court has now converted it into a legal principle, and applied it to driving. Reviewing an appeal of a drunk driving case, the justices ruled that the state's drunken driving law could be applied to an intoxicated person found in the driver's seat of a vehicle, even though the car was parked and not moving, as long as the key was in the ignition.

Wouldn't it have been easier to pass a law against drunk parking?

⚖

In the fall of 1992, M.C. Ren, member of that fun-loving group of gangsta rappers, NWA (Niggers With Attitudes), was served with a paternity suit by a woman who claimed that she had been raped by Ren in 1989, when she was 16. Ren originally settled out of court, agreeing to pay the woman $350,000. The rest of the group was not as eager to go along with the deal and tried to have the agreement thrown out or reduced.

Sensing that the rappers didn't get the point the first time, the judge then ordered each of the four rappers in the group to kick in $2 million individually and another $8 million from their business empire. Kind of puts the $350,000 in perspective.

⚖

More than 30,000 fans watched Probe and Park Avenue Joe finish the 1989 Hambletonian, the Kentucky Derby of harness racing, in a dead heat. Few that day would have suspected that the race would eventually end in a court room.

Lindy Farms of Connecticut, the owners of Probe, sued for half of the winnings and to overturn the ruling of the New Jersey Race Commission, which had declared the horses co-winners for the record books, but gave the majority of the purse to Park Avenue Joe based on a better showing in preliminary heats. George Cohen of the Racing Commission said that "the rules had somewhat vague language regarding the winner versus the winning share of the purse." Local bookies have yet to post a line on the outcome of the suit.

⚖

Calling abortion one of the "most profound issues of our time" and the law "the greatest teacher known to mankind," Harold J. Cassidy presented a suit before the New Jersey Supreme Court asking it to determine when life begins. If they can decide that, maybe they can determine where socks go when they disappear.

In October of 1992 the U.S. Supreme Court refused to hear the appeal of a New Jersey man represented by Cassidy who was trying to stop his girlfriend from having an abortion.

⚖

Remember this name: Laurence H. Adler. A real trailblazer, Mr. Adler is the first person in the country to be criminally prosecuted for cheating on his Scholastic Aptitude Test. The criminal charges stemmed from a suit that Adler brought against the

Educational Testing Service in an effort to prevent them from cancelling his fraudulent scores.

Adler paid a friend $200 to take his college boards. That friend lost his scholarship and was dismissed from college when the case came to light. A Maryland judge sentenced Adler to six months in jail, three years of supervised probation and 100 hours of community service. All this just because he wanted to go to Syracuse?

⚖️

In the mid-'70's, a high school student sued her gym teacher and the city of Bristol, Connecticut after breaking her finger trying to catch a pop fly in a school softball game. The girl alleged that her teacher failed to instruct her adequately in the art of catching a pop fly. She also claims that he failed to warn her about the dangers of playing the outfield.

⚖️

A lawsuit filed in Grayson County, Texas alleges that a Dallas mortuary college and 35 North Texas funeral homes and embalming centers "conspired and participated in an arrangement where the bodies of deceased persons were obtained and used for instructional purposes...." The suit requested an unspecified amount for alleged fraud, negligence, deceptive trade practices and breach of contract.

John Cathey, executive director of the Texas

Funeral Directors Association, said that the funeral homes involved believed that by obtaining relatives' permission to embalm a body they also obtained permission for students to assist in the process if they are supervised by a licensed embalmer. There was no opinion available from the deceased.

⚖

Demonstrating that the spirit of the Wild West is still very much alive, the Colorado Attorney's Office and four Denver residents have filed a suit in Denver asking the court to overturn that city's ordinance from banning the sale of semi-automatic assault weapons.

Assistant Attorney General David Kopel said that the Denver City Council had "denigrated the right to self defense" by passing the ordinance. Kopel contended that the ordinance had taken away guns that are superior for self defense. "The constitution does not require use of inferior weapons for self defense," he said.

⚖

New York attorney Ariel Vista filed a $65 million class action lawsuit on behalf of the Congress of Filipino American Citizens against radio personality Howard Stern. Stern allegedly made several slanderous remarks about the Philippines during a September 1992 broadcast including, "I think they eat their young over there."

Calling the $65 million sought in the suit "a symbolic amount," Vista said the figure represents the number of Filipinos around the world. "We only charged Stern $1 per person, which is very cheap, considering the amount of damage he has inflicted on our people."

⚖

The Kentucky State Department of Insurance sued a group of insurance companies for operating without a license. The companies were also accused of marketing "rapture insurance" which would pay benefits to survivors in the event that 1 million or more people disappeared from the planet.

The rapture is described in the Bible as an event that will occur prior to the end of the world, at which time believers will be taken physically into heaven. And if your survivors are left behind to receive the benefit, they can at least afford to enjoy themselves in hell.

⚖

In what promises to be a thorny legal question, the Arizona Court of Appeals ruled that H.B. and Jocelyn Wallace of Scottsdale, Arizona were denied due process when authorities attempted to remove eight crested saguaro cactus plants, worth over $30,000, from their property. The Wallaces contend that when they purchased the saguaros in 1989 the cacti had valid state tags which allowed them to be sold and planted on private property.

The state Agriculture Department wants to seize

the plants under the Arizona Native Plants Act, which requires anyone who wants to remove protected plants from their natural setting to get permission from the owner of the property.

⚖

In a lawsuit filed in New Jersey, four families sued the Roman Catholic Diocese of Trenton and their local parish priest claiming that they lost their faith, and with it their chance to go to heaven, after their parish priest sexually assaulted their four daughters.

While the families sought monetary damages, no exact financial value was placed on the loss of faith or the inability to get into heaven.

⚖

In a step that surely was taken for the collective good, the Italian American Society of America sued the U. S. Postal Service in 1976 in order to prevent them from issuing a stamp that would have commemorated Alexander Graham Bell as the inventor of the telephone.

They have evidence that it was really invented by one Antonio Meucci.

⚖

In a case that could end up in the Insurance Hall of Fame, a Minnesota jury awarded $2.4 million in damages to a young woman who sued her father for sexually molesting her, and her mother for ignoring the abuse. The jury deliberated for two hours before returning the verdict, which included a negligence finding against the mother.

The young woman's attorney said that a claim would be made against the mother's homeowner's insurance in an attempt to recover the damages.

⚖

Jason Pickney, described as a body building extra, was awarded $487,500 by a Fayetteville, N.C. jury for injuries he suffered during a fight scene while filming the movie *Cyborg.*

Pickney claims that he was hit in the eye by a prop knife wielded by actor Jean Claude Van Damme, who was trying to make the scene more realistic. Maybe he should stick to musicals from now on.

⚖

Federal district judge ruled that the state of Indiana is not obligated to provide estrogen treatments to a 27-year-old convicted murderer incarcerated in a state facility. In an effort to become female, the inmate has already undergone chemical castration, breast implants and silicone injections. He also wears women's clothing.

Prison officials have classified the inmate as male because of his genitalia and have kept him away from the general prison population. The court found that the failure on the part of the state to provide additional treatment does not constitute cruel and unusual punishment. Maybe not to him, but you can bet that the rest of the guys in the joint are disappointed.

⚖️

Jailed hotel regent Leona Helmsley is being sued for $5 million by her former chef, James Houlihan. Houlihan claims that he wrecked his knee by falling on slush that came from Helmsley's freezer and not, as one might have assumed, from her heart.

Helmsley's response upon hearing about the suit: "Why are you doing this to me now?" That's easy, Leona. Because you can't fire him now.

⚖️

A student sued Gonzaga University after flunking out of its Law School. She asked for either $110,000 or a law degree on the grounds that, given her poor college grades and weak showing on the law boards, Gonzaga should have told her that she didn't have much of a chance of making it in law school.

Don't know about the cash, but the quality of her argument certainly merits a law degree.

⚖️

The Pennsylvania Supreme Court may finally have provided us with a legal definition of when enough is enough when it ruled that divorced or separated parents are not legally responsible for financing their children's college education.

Writing in the 5-1 decision, Justice Stephen A. Zappala said that "a parental duty of support is owed until the child is 18 or graduated from high school, which ever event occurs later. This will ensure that children have a minimum education to prepare them for the challenges of life." Clearly the words of a man who has never set foot in public school.

⚖

A federal appeals court has ruled that former president Richard Nixon, the Energizer Bunny of American politics, is entitled to compensation for his presidential papers and tapes that are still under government control. One appraiser has estimated that the tapes and papers could be worth between $1.5 million and $2.5 million. Who knows how much more he'd get for the Director's Cut of the Watergate tapes, which runs eighteen-and-a-half minutes longer than the regular release.

Clearly, their value is of a different order than those of president Chester A. Arthur, who burned his papers in three large garbage cans upon leaving office.

⚖

After 11 years of marriage, Bonnette Askew finally admitted that she had never been romantically attracted to her husband, Ronald. Ronald responded with a lawsuit claiming that Bonette had defrauded him. Bonette claimed that she didn't tell her husband because she didn't want to hurt his male ego. A Santa Ana, California jury agreed with Ronald and awarded him $242,000 in damages.

Seems like the jury got it backwards -- if it took Ronald 11 years to notice, Bonette should have received the award. The Academy Award.

⚖

Fearing what they called the dilution of the distinctive quality of their name, Hell's Angels sued Marvel Comics asking it to change the name of Marvel's newest comic book character, a superhuman woman named Hell's Angel.

The "exclusive and elite organization of motorcycle enthusiasts" claimed that the comic caused "public confusion" between the comic book and the cycle club. They asked for an immediate halt to Marvel's use of the name, the destruction of all comic books as well as monetary damages. Maybe it's not the public who's confused, after all.

⚖

A federal jury in Miami, Florida ruled that it is a violation of your civil rights to have a firefighter rub his scrotum on your forehead. The jury then went on to reward rookie firefighter Herman Skinner $1.3 million in a judgment against the city of Miami. The city had turned down an offer to settle out of court.

Skinner sued the city after being subjected to the traditional hazing (packing genitals on ice, soaking

28

clothes in blood) that rookies are subjected to by veteran firefighters. In Skinner's case, he was handcuffed and held to the ground while his supervisor applied the costly scrotum rub.

⚖

Challenging the Bush Administration to make its tax code consistent with its family values, Andrea Cassman sued the U.S. government, claiming that she should be able to deduct her unborn child on her federal tax return. Cassman claims that Jonathan Cassman, the fetus in question, became her child at the time of conception and that she should be eligible for an appropriate deduction.

IRS officials were able to identify only one other suit attempting to claim an unborn child as an exemption. That suit was rejected. Cassman's claim could, however, pave the way for the "glimmer in the eye" or "lust in the heart" exemptions.

⚖

The New York State Court of Appeals declared that customers of live peep shows must pay state sales tax. Customers of these "fantasy booths" observe a show performed by women dressed in "abbreviated attire" by dropping coins in a device that controls a partition that separates the performer from the patron's view.

A group of sex show operators located in New York City's Times Square area had argued that the peep shows are controlled by a token-triggered device which makes them more like jukeboxes, which are not taxed. The court, in a classic example of legal understatement, ruled that the peep shows can be taxed because they are a form of live entertainment.

⚖

Anne Hiltner, a self-described unpublished romance writer who lives with her mother, sued Stephen King, claiming that he broke into either her home or her storage space in either 1986 or '87 and stole eight copyrighted manuscripts written by either herself or her brother. Included in the eight was the best-seller, *Misery.*

Hiltner, claiming to be the real Annie Wilkes of the book and movie, has asked for undisclosed damages, a share in the profits and the removal of the book from stores. Seems like it would have been easier to have the judge declare her to be Stephen King.

"You can't go around hitting people, so the only thing you can do is sue."

James Blakely, 38, of Detroit, has sued the Detroit Newspaper Agency, claiming that the horoscopes printed in their papers were to blame for an "enormous amount of problems" in his life, including his failed marriage.

Astrologer Sydney Omar, who writes the horoscope column that appears in the papers, said that he foresaw the outcome of the suit in January. Mr. Blakely is reported to be a Leo.

In the ultimate definition of a bad hair day, Eric S. Graham sued J. C. Penny for over $10,000 in damages, claiming that the haircut he received from their styling salon in Orlando, Florida left him "ashamed and ridiculed" and deprived him of his right to enjoy life.

No doubt something the framers of the constitution must have overlooked.

Graham's suit claims that it took him two and a half years to grow his hair to the desired length, and that he had to undergo psychiatric treatment in order to control the panic anxiety disorder that resulted from the haircut.

Kevin Ross sued Creighton University, claiming that Creighton exploited his athletic ability and failed to educate him while he played basketball for the University in the early 1980's. When he left school, Ross was 36 hours short of graduation and unable to read at the high school level.

While admitting no liability in the case, Creighton agreed to settle out of court for $30,000. Ross is probably lucky that Creighton didn't institute a counter-suit against him for failing to make it to the Final Four. Or for failing to make it to the library, for that matter.

Claiming that Utah owns its wildlife and is responsible when one of its animals acts up, a 34-year old Minnesota man sued the state to cover $2,000 in medical treatment for injuries suffered when a coyote gnawed on his head and neck while he slept outside at an I-80 rest stop near Green River, Utah.

Apparently no insomniac, the man admitted that

he saw the coyote but thought that it had left the area before he went to sleep.

In a $50,000 suit for "false imprisonment", Pamela Leigh sued Republic Parking for "undue mental distress" that resulted from being locked in a downtown Atlanta parking garage on the eve of the long Labor Day weekend. The gates to the garage had been locked at 7:15pm instead of their usual 8:00pm.

After screaming for help for approximately 45 minutes, Ms. Leigh escaped by jumping from the garage to the ground below. According to her attorney, Ms. Leigh "doesn't like enclosed garages anymore."

Proving that some folks still have pride in a job well done, Kevin Barry brought suit against the federal government demanding that it classify the money he received through panhandling as earned income rather than as unearned gifts. He claimed that the unearned gifts classification reduced his disability benefits.

Panhandling is not an easy job, according to Barry: "I would stand at a busy intersection under a traffic light. When the cars stopped for the red light, I would walk down the line of cars and ask for money.... When the light turned green I would walk back to the traffic light and wait for the light to turn red again." His attorney called panhandling a trade, comparing it to raising funds for the Rockefeller Foundation.

The U. S. Supreme Court has ruled that frightened passengers can't claim damages for being scared to death or other emotional distress when they are riding on a turbulent flight if the plane in question doesn't crash. Alex Embry and 24 other passengers brought suit against Eastern Airlines after experiencing 10 minutes of what they called sheer terror on a flight from Miami to the Bahamas. The plane lost oil pressure and the crew started to inform the passengers that they may have to crash into the Atlantic Ocean.

"It was a horrible experience," said Embry "It still bothers me to fly. Every time there's turbulence I break out in a cold sweat." Unfortunately for Embry, the Supreme Court does not equate a cold sweat with bodily harm. That is, unless your plane crashes.

Chief Rabbi Michael Shane Sofer, the True King of Israel of God, AkA the Great Prince Michael, a resident of North Carolina, has been working a day job as "Messenger of the Covenant of Promise, clearly identified by the authority of Almighty God and all His Holy Prophets, since the world began." In 1990, he sued Ronald Reagan, George Bush and the United States of America for supporting the Zionist State of

Israel, which is located in an area he considers his personal property.

When filing his claim, Great Prince Michael listed God as his employer. Apparently, the Almighty has yet to hear of minimum wage, since the Great Prince listed his salary as "none," and asked to have his filing fees waived. The court complied with his request.

Motown magnate Berry Gordy was sued by a Washington man who accused Gordy of tapping into his brain and siphoning off all of Motown's hits, including the work of Diana Ross, the Jackson 5 and Sammy Davis, Jr. The man wasn't too proud to beg, and offered to settle for a cool $20 million.

Gordy was also sued by a California man who claimed that Mr. Gordy stole his name and gave it to Michael Jackson. Jackson (the suer, not the singer) requested Gordy's Hollywood mansion as settlement. Jackson also sued the Los Angeles Lakers basketball team for $7 million, claiming that Magic Johnson had stolen his phallus.

Some law suits are inter-stellar in nature. David Ward claimed in a Texas court that he designed *Star Trek's* Starship Enterprise. Not being a greedy fellow, he demanded the following compensation: $500 million in cash, 500 acres of land, a truck, a car and a 30-foot speed boat.

At the bottom of the filing, Ward scribbled, "This might seem like a lot but it is considerably less than the $750 mil I was asking for."

Maybe it's the water in Texas that starts folks thinking big. A prisoner there was sure that the State Attorney had done him wrong, and sued the Attorney General for $5 trillion. Not wanting to mess with middle men, the prisoner represented himself and claimed that he was entitled to reclaim legal fees which he calculated at the modest sum of $100,000 an hour.

A considerate sort, the prisoner asked that half the money be deposited in a trust fund and the other half be given to his mother. Just to make it easy on everyone, he included several deposit slips with his filing.

On the evening of December 22, 1989, Mr. James Crangle found himself driving the wrong way down a one-way street in our nation's capitol (hey, it happens). Upon spotting Mr. Crangle, the District Police gave chase. He tried to elude them and ended up ramming his car into a utility pole. In an effort to avoid arrest, he climbed on top of a mailbox where he claimed sanctuary, literally.

After his arrest, Mr. Crangle filed a suit listed as

James Crangle - Citizen v. District of Columbia - Police State Leviathan, in which he claimed that the district police had no authority to arrest him since he was on federal property, the mailbox, at the time of the arrest. After a lengthy hearing, the suit was dismissed.

In 1987 in Martinez, California, war protestors attempted to prevent a Navy train from reaching a local munitions depot by lying on the railroad tracks. After some haggling, the train proceeded, severing the legs of a protestor.

Distraught over the event, several of the more sensitive members of the train's crew sued the now-legless protestor for creating a situation which caused them to experience post traumatic stress disorder.

Edward H. Winter of Cincinnati was a man who knew exactly what he wanted. While in the hospital, he experienced extremely rapid heartbeat. Hospital staff responded by taking emergency measures to save his life, despite his clear instructions that they were not to take such steps in the event such an emergency occurred.

Winter responded with a "wrongful living " law suit, suing the staff for disregarding his wishes. When he passed away two years later, the suit lived on, pursued by his estate.

Tom Morgan was a cashier in a suburban Portland, Oregon grocery store. According to Morgan, fellow cashier Randy Maresh lived to torment him. Each day. Every day. Morgan sued Maresh for $100,000 on the grounds that he "willfully and maliciously inflicted severe mental stress and humiliation....by continually, intentionally and repeatedly passing gas directed at the plaintiff."

Maresh's attorney's held that breaking wind is a form of free speech and thus is protected by the first amendment. The judge, despite finding Maresh's behavior "juvenile and boorish," could find no law against it and dismissed the case.

In September of 1978, Emma McDougald fell into a coma after a Caesarean section. Her family sued her doctors for the usual pain and suffering, kind of like the compulsory figures section of the event, and then went into the freestyle phase: they sued for hedonic damages. Loosely translated, this means they sued for McDougald's inability to experience joy as a result of the coma. The jury awarded $1 million for the suffering and $3.5 million for the loss of pleasure.

The second award was tossed out by the New York State Supreme Court. The Court reasoned that lawyers can still claim loss of joy only if the victim is aware enough to experience the loss. The ruling was written by chief Judge Sol Wachtler, who has recently received much public attention for his overzealous pursuit of joy of the extramarital kind.

When Christopher Duffy of Framingham, Massachusettes stole a car from a parking lot, he didn't get very far. There was an accident and Mr. Duffy shuffled off this mortal coil, leaving behind an estate.

The estate, driven by a Barnumesque understanding of the material world, sued the proprietor of the parking lot for failing to prevent car thefts.

Boyd L. Davis got a bit testy when he discovered that a produce clerk had overcharged him for a five-pound bag of apples. Enraged, Davis hurled the apples at the clerk. His aim, however was about as accurate as the clerk's math. The errant fruit bounced off of the head of one Mary Lou Settle, your garden variety innocent bystander.

Ms. Settle decided that she wouldn't (settle that is), and sued Davis for $1 million to cover medical care for head injuries and ongoing pain.

He's the Lou Gehrig of litigation, the sultan of suits, the Edsel of evidence. He is Alfred Spremo, Jr. and in the last 17 years he has sued his neighbor, a mattress maker, a child care agency, a repo agency, a video repair shop, his own lawyer, 30 state and federal judges... he even sued Mom. His legal philosophy? "You can't go around hitting people, so the only thing you can do is sue."

In 1986, his mother nearly severed his ring finger by accidently slamming the cellar door on it. Mr. Spremo, now aged 57, sued her. And when he couldn't come to an agreement over his attorney's legal fees (after settling with his mother's insurance company for $4,000) he sued his lawyer, his mother's insurance company and its lawyer. Spremo may have filed his last complaint in New York State, however -- the state supreme court has ordered that he never again sue anyone in the state.

The world don't need no more womens with PhD's in English. At least that appears to be the sentiment of attorney Douglas Page. Page sued to have his ex-wife dismissed from her graduate school studies, arguing that such activities are frivolous. He claimed that during their seven years of marriage, Mrs. Page had not held a job but had managed to have six different academic majors.

It takes more than a mere secular tribunal to command filial devotion." And with those words, Judge Anthony Scariano denied the appeal of Mrs. Rosenbaum, better known as Richard's mother. In 1985 Richard Rosenbaum went to court and got an order that legally prevented his mother from calling him and his wife. It was part of a package deal that directed Richard to call his mother every three months and meet her in person at least once a year.

The court eventually dropped Richard's legal obligation to call and visit with mom. That's when Richard's mother, who lives within minutes of her son's home, appealed in an attempt to have the order reinstated. She lost.

Ladies and Gentlemen. In this corner we have Hasbro Industries, makers of that deadly killing machine, G.I. Joe. Hasbro was willing to argue to anyone who would listen that G.I. Joe was a toy soldier and not, well you know, a doll. And in this corner we have the U.S. Customs Service who were of the opinion that Mr. Joe was indeed a doll and, as such, should be subject to the import tariffs that are imposed on dolls.

The debate was settled by a three-judge panel that decided no matter how butch he looked, Hasbro's defender of democracy and the American way of life was still, well, you know, a doll.

Did you hear the one about the blind woman who took her dog to the movies? Lowes Orpheum Theatre in New York City did. In 1987 Madeline Silver and her guide dog, Joy, were turned away from the theatre when they tried to see a James Bond film. The theatre manager said that Silver didn't look blind

41

and that he thought that she was "just trying to take her dog to the movies." And you thought New Yorkers were jaded.

Silver settled out of court for $7,000, which will buy a lot of popcorn even in Manhattan, and the Orpheum's agreement to post signs that guarantee that they will not discriminate against disabled people. No word on whether or not the signs are in Braille.

And in another canine caper, Master Teddy won't have to get a tattoo after all. Celeste Crawford directed in her will that Master Teddy, her 13 year old dog, could live in Crawford's $102,000 Maryland home, complete with caretaker, for the rest of his life. Six of Crawford's human heirs have contested the will on several occasions. They are of the opinion that, with Master Teddy in residence, selling the property could take them forever, even measured in dog years.

In a recent attempt to make sure that the caretaker or anyone else didn't try to drag out the process by kidnapping or replacing Master Teddy with a younger imposter, they tried to get a Maryland judge to order that Crawford's non-human heir should be tattooed by a veterinarian in order to prove that he is the original Master Teddy. Who knows -- maybe something tasteful, like a little heart with "Celeste" in the center.

George Schnable, the dog's caretaker, protested that the tattooing would subject Teddy to a traumatic experience. Schnable and the human heirs eventually reached a legally-binding compromise under which Master Teddy would by X-rayed and those X-rays would be monitored on a regular basis in order to prove that he was the one and only Master Teddy.

Adam Cooperman wanted to attend the U.S. Navel Academy, but was worried that the D+ that he had received in advanced calculus might prevent him from being admitted. So he did what any enterprising young man would do: he got the court to issue temporary restraining order that prevented school officials from including the D+ in his transcript when it was sent to the Academy as part of his application.

His parents agreed with his approach. They claimed that a case of tonsillitis forced him to hand in his homework late, and that's what caused the low grade. School officials disagreed and so did Judge Bob N. Krug, who lifted the restraining order. Krug said that withholding the grade amounted to "hoodwinking" the academy.

When is a moon not a moon? The Utah Court of Appeals answered that piece of social astronomy when it ruled that Marie Serrente could not be prosecuted under the state's criminal lewdness law. In April of 1986, Serrente visited her son's algebra teacher. After an argument over whether or not her son was a discipline problem, Serrente raised her dress upon leaving the class room and said, "To you, sir." Serrente was tried and convicted of criminal lewdness with the court holding that she had directed public attention to her private body parts, which is actionable as lewdness in Utah.

The appeals court decided to turn the other legal cheek, as it were, and throw out the conviction since Serrente had worn underwear. Witnesses agreed that no naked skin was observable during the incident, which convinced the court to declare that the moon had not been legally visible that day. Or at least not enough to constitute lewdness.

Who says that the folks in Palm Beach County don't care about family values? Darleen Scott's neighbor, a male neighbor, just happened to be glancing in the window of her third floor apartment when he was scandalized by what he claimed was the sight of Scott dancing nude in front of her two children. He did what any concerned male neighbor who just happened to be glancing in a third story window would do. He filed a child abuse report with the police. Scott was arrested and her daughters, ages 3 and 10, were sent to separate foster homes.

Scott, with the help of the ACLU, responded with a suit for false arrest, harassment and false imprisonment against the Palm Beach Safety Department. While she doesn't deny dancing, she claims that she had wrapped herself in a towel upon leaving the shower so she could catch her favorite Gladys Knight video on television. The video? *Love Overboard.*

A picture may be worth a thousand words, but to attorney James A. Sposito they were the wrong words. Words like "ambulance chaser," or "doofus." It seems that Sposito had paid for an advertisement in the Donnelly Directory and had included an illustration of crashed vehicles that he thought communicated his speciality, personal injury law, in a dramatic manner. Unfortunately for Sposito, the crashed vehicles in the ad were ambulances.

He sued the publisher of the phone book for defamation of character and breach of contract. They countered with a motion for dismissal, claiming that the photo that Sposito had selected first had an ambulance in it anyway. Sposito's attorney said that he has received numerous calls from other attorneys, "who phone just to laugh at him."

Declaring that the lawsuit didn't change his opinion of their music, rock music critic Charles Eddy filed a $500,000 suit for damages against those charmers of rap, the Beastie Boys. Just prior to the suit, Eddy had included one of their albums on his list of Top Ten Favorites. The suit alleges that the Beastie Boys committed battery and invaded his privacy.

More specifically, what they invaded was his West Hollywood hotel room at 2:30 in the morning, where they proceeded to pour buckets of water on his head. Maybe they hadn't heard about the top ten list. They also filmed the escapade without his permission and included it in a music video. Eddy found out about his featured role in the video after a friend purchased it.

Justice F. Douglas McDaniel proved that the third time really is a charm. The judge was accused of slapping one 12-year-old boy and choking another 12-year-old after warning them three times to stop laughing during a screening of the movie *Pretty Woman*.

Justice McDaniel avoided disciplinary action by reaching an out-of-court settlement with the kids' families. He continues to hear a full load of cases and is on active senior status with the Fourth District Court of Appeals.

For those of you who have always wondered what goes into an attorney's billable hour, Chicagoan Sherry Kantar could shed some light on the subject. The $15,000 bill that she received from her attorney for handling her divorce included the time that they spent having sex.

It took Kantar eleven weeks to file a complaint

against her attorney, Albert Brooks Friedman. A Chicago appeals court ruled that, despite the fact this was longer than usual, it was permissible in this case since she had to find a new lawyer. During that same eleven-week period, Friedman was named staff to the Illinois Supreme Court's Committee on Character and Fitness.

Attorney Robert McKim Norris, Jr. sent a flower wreath and a sympathy card to the parents of a toddler who had died while being watched by a daycare center. That's okay. What's not okay, according to the Alabama Supreme Court, was including a brochure that described his law firm and gave his business phone number. That's called soliciting for pecuniary gain and goes beyond the bounds of the state's disciplinary rules, not to mention the bounds of civilized society.

Norris took his case to the state supreme court, saying in his argument that the rules were too vague, at least to him.

Tom Hanson, 25, of Boulder, Colorado thought that his parents were guilty of what he called "willful and wanton neglect." So he sued them for $350,000. Hanson described his legal action as a "suit of malpractice of parenting."

Perseverance. That's what Marlene Swimley of Chicago had. Perseverance. Swimley hired a hit man to kill her husband. The plot was foiled and Swimley was convicted on criminal charges.

That didn't stop her, though. She then hired a lawyer to put a legal hit on her husband for $500 permanent alimony and the title to the couple's $250,000 home.

In the case of yet another topless dancer fighting discrimination, Cynthia Logan of Denver, Colorado went to court to demand her job back from the bar where she had been dancing. After all, she argued, just because she was seven months pregnant it didn't mean that she couldn't fulfill her professional and artistic responsibilities.

Maybe they wanted to make sure that you didn't get the wrong idea from their slogan, "Nothin' says lovin' like somethin' from the oven." Maybe they wanted to make sure that the only thing rising was the dough. Whatever the reason, Pillsbury wasn't about to take any chances, so it sued Screw magazine publisher Al Goldstein for $1.5 million because of a parody that appeared in Screw that showed Poppin' Fresh and his companion Poppie Fresh doing the wild thing in a skillet.

A kiss might just be a kiss, but a federal court ruling said an engagement ring is more than a "mere ornament." The judge defined it as "necessary wearing apparel" and as an item of "great sentimental value." That meant that the wife of a bankrupt California businessman could keep the $10,000 ring. The businessman wanted to include the ring in the tally of the couple's jointly-held financial assets.

Another entrant in the "suits we would all like to file" category is the couple from Louisiana who sued South Central Bell Telephone Company. Their beef? The telephone repairman failed to show up as scheduled, and you know where that can lead. First came the "terrible mood" and then the family squabbles followed by the canned chili dinner and the group depression. The only way to alleviate that was a weekend trip to the Big Easy, which set them back $500, the sum for which they sued.

Yet another convict has tried to bring a new dimension to the constitution's provision against cruel and unusual punishment. Ralph Dodson, a resident of one of Indiana's finest institutions, argued unsuccessfully in his lawsuit that keeping him locked up with men and away from women was indeed cruel and unusual. He requested a transfer to a women's prison.

Some folks are just incredibly unluckily. Take Carl Fetterman, for instance. Fetterman sued a candy maker after finding a piece of glass in a candy bar that he had started to consume. You might think that that was bad luck, but imagine having something like that happen to you on at least nine different occasions with different food products over a two-year period. And imagine having to settle out of court for $5,000 in at least one instance. Wow!

U.S. Attorney Robert Nolan thought that the story was just a little incredible, and made sure that the jury in the candy bar case was informed about Fetterman's streak of bad luck. They threw out the case, but hung on to Fetterman who was later found guilty of communicating false information in a consumer products investigation.

Carole Van Zeeland and her husband, Gary, were on safari in Zimbabwe when a bull elephant charged, picked her up in his trunk and spun her around. As a result of this display of prehensile pachyderm dexterity, Mrs. Van Zeeland suffered several broken bones. She sued him for her injuries. Not the elephant, but her husband, who is a big game hunter. She claimed, in a $1,000,000 suit filed in Outgamie County, Wisconsin, that he was negligent by going out on the hunt armed with nothing but a camera.

The jury agreed and awarded her a trophy in the amount of $250,000 which was to be paid by her husband's insurer.

I n times of crisis we tend to rely on what we know best. Take Chicago Judge Margaret O'Malley, who fell and landed on her elbow when leaving her official bench. She spent several weeks in the hospital nursing the wounded elbow and when she was released she sued the courthouse for $150,000 for allegedly failing to meet the building code.

T he official court records in San Francisco, California clearly showed that James Russell was convicted of a felony and that he had to serve 15 months in state prison. The only problem was that the official records were wrong. Russell was really convicted of a misdemeanor and should have done only 83 days of county time.

Russell sued and was awarded $100,000 in what might be described as overtime pay.

C arol Gagnon held the thankless job of school cafeteria cook for only six weeks before she was fired. That didn't stop her and her husband, James, from suing the school for libel. It seems that an article written by the 10th and 11th graders for the school newspaper had described Mrs. Gagnon's cooking as "not fit for dogs to eat." They also claimed they had found hair in the food.

The New York Supreme Court upheld the honor

of Mrs. Gagnon and of school cafeteria cooks everywhere when they awarded her $10,000 in damages. Just for the record, the article appeared after she had been fired.

Michael Denardo got a bit testy when the coffee machine at work ate his money, then didn't deliver. So he gave it a whack. All he got for his trouble was a 10% loss of the use of his right hand. Denardo sued for workman's compensation and the Rhode Island Supreme Court agreed with him. They were probably wearing "Death Before Decaf" T-shirts under those robes.

"I guess I'd better stick to medicine, because I sure don't understand the judicial system."

Johanna A. Ramo sued her cable television company and the FCC in an effort to have the cable company turn its cables off. Ramo complained that the wires were leaking into her home which caused "her smile to disappear" and "her brain cells to dry up." A condition no doubt familiar to many TV viewers.

In addition, she reported that she kept hearing songs in her head. The theme to Jeopardy, perhaps?

It cost Michael Clemens $75,000 to take the law into his own hands. Seems that he caught Francis Rakowski in the act of burglarizing his car, and chased him for two hours. He finally fired a warning shot which hit Rakowski in the foot. "They ruined the rest of my life, because I'm a crippled person now," said Rakowski, who was convicted on the burglary charge, but sued Clemens anyhow. Apparently the jury agreed, significantly supplementing the $150 Rakowski netted from the heist.

Rakowski was convicted two years later of stealing a car. During that episode, he was able to walk more than a mile, ruined life and all.

Those wacky inmates are at it again. This time, three residents of the Orleans Parish Prison sued a local television station for $75,000 in damages resulting from a change in the viewing schedule. It seems that the station had advertised that they were to show *The Split*, a movie about a prison escape. As a community service, the inmates told their fellow prisoners about this special viewing opportunity.

Imagine their chagrin and surprise when the station broadcast the movie *Warlock Moon*, instead. The inmates claimed damages for "false advertising, mental anguish, embarrassment and the destruction of excitement, happiness and joy." Case dismissed.

Don't be so stupid". That's what Wendy Tillotson's teacher told her when she tried to decline a turn at the hurdles in gym. Wendy, age 11, jumped and broke her leg. She went to the hospital and gained 70

pounds. As she put it, "There were boxes of chocolates piling up -- so I ate them."

As a result, a London judge ordered a local school district to pay Wendy $13,000 in damages....for the weight gain. "She is entitled to compensation for the fact that she became so grossly overweight, which certainly made her look less attractive," said Judge William Mars-Jones.

Kazunari Ignarashi was mildly miffed when Madonna canceled her scheduled concert date in Tokyo. So he sued for $73 to cover his mental anguish. But that wasn't all. As part of the action, he also wanted the Material Girl to schedule a new date. The court ruled that since it couldn't physically force Madonna to sing, the demand was not enforceable.

Rick L. Gibbons of Council Bluffs, Iowa sued the American Bowling Congress because it refused to certify his perfect game, even though the West Lanes Bowling Center issued him a check for bowling a perfect score of 300. It seems that the inspector for the Omaha Men's Bowling Association cast aspersions on Gibbons' date with perfection when he found that the Bowling Center had coated their lanes with mineral oil. As we all know, this sort of application violates regulations, and so the ABC decided not to cheapen the degree by issuing a certificate to Gibbons under what they considered to be questionable circumstances.

Frank and Mary Jean Kranack of Pittsburgh, Pennsylvania sued Domino's Pizza after their station wagon was hit broadside by a pizza delivery person trying to live up to Domino's guarantee of delivery in 30 minutes or the pizza is on them. Instead, it was on the Kranacks and their vehicle. Mrs. Kranack claimed that she suffered permanent disability in her right arm as a result of the accident, while her husband experienced whiplash.

The stroke that really put the final anchovy on the legal pie, however, was when the driver's manager appeared at the scene of the accident and screamed, "Let's get this pizza on the road!" The Kranacks sued for an unspecified slice of Domino's assets.

It wasn't exactly a call from the governor, but it did take a ruling from a circuit court judge to save Max from the gas chamber. His crime? Barking. Max, a three-year-old mixed breed, had been sentenced to death by a district judge in Norfolk, Virginia after neighbors complained to the court that he barked too much.

Tom Atkinson, Max's owner, went to the higher court to get the stay of execution. As part of the agreement, Max, who did not have to testify, will have to undergo training to learn how to be quiet .

Robert Couf, a martial arts student in Broward County, Florida sued Michael LaMedica for allegedly attacking him in an altercation over a parking space. LaMedica's weapon? His chin.

Couf claimed that he suffered a broken hand when he administered a karate chop aimed at LaMedica's chin. So, of course, Couf sued for damages, presumably to his ego as well as to his hand. LaMedica is 20 years his senior.

In more consumer news, Baskin-Robbins, makers of Pralines 'N Cream ice cream, sued Pillsbury, the makers of Häagen-Daz ice cream, for damages resulting from "unfair competition." They thought Häagen-Daz's new flavor, Pralines & Cream, infringed on their trademark-protected product. Not to mention that it might confuse the unwary consumer.

Baskin-Robbins also thought that Pillsbury/ Häagen-Daz was engaging in misleading advertising by printing the words "Oslo & Copenhagen" on the outside of their packages. To Baskin-Robbins, this indicated that Pillsbury wanted consumers to think that their product is made in Scandinavia. Baskin-Robbins attorney Charles McConachie was quick to point out that

Häagen-Daz is actually made in New Jersey.
Copenhagen, New Jersey?

He didn't want to be picky, but David Jackson thought that he might deserve a new trial, so he filed an appeal. Convicted of two felonies and sentenced to five years, Jackson didn't find out until after his trial that his attorney was dating the Deputy District Attorney who put him away .

His new attorney, Henry Zall, put it all in context when he said, "Sometimes I've suspected the defense to be in bed with the prosecution, but I have never seen a case where it seemed to be literally true."

Back in the mid-80's, an Olympic torch was worth about $3,000 on the open market. However, when the Pacifica and South City Boys and Girls Club couldn't get the torch back from one of their runners, they upped the ante to $50,000 in damages in a suit against Tonya Elkins and her family. 7-year old Tonya had carried the torch in a pre-Olympic ceremony. After the ceremony she refused to give it up.

Tonya's mom said that she was never told that Tonya had to surrender the torch. Club officials said that they told her twice that the torch was club property. Before the burning issue could be settled, Mrs. Elkins announced that she was counter-suing for emotional distress and invasion of privacy. All in the spirit of brotherhood and fair play.

The free caffeine will continue to flow in the Iowa court system, thanks to a ruling of the Iowa Court of Appeals. A convicted burglar sued for a reversal of his conviction on the grounds that the practice of giving free coffee to jurors might prejudice them in favor of the prosecutor.

The parents of a 20-year old Hackensack, New Jersey man asked the court to banish him from their household, and Judge Sherwin Lester complied. According to his parents, Michael A. Stott refused to work and spent all day planted in front of the television, drinking beer and just generally serving as a bad example for the five other kids in the family.

Royston Potter thought that he was "living the principle" and that Murray, Utah had no right to kick him off of the police force for having three wives. He didn't see his arrangement as a matter of choice. "It's necessary as far as a [Mormon] theology goes," said Potter.

So he sued the city, charging that the dismissal was a violation of his privacy. He also claimed that he was denied due process since criminal charges for practicing polygamy were never lodged against him.

Nancy Paulson of Great Falls, Montana sued the Crescent Food snack company and a local supermarket for misrepresentation, negligence, breach of implied warranty of fitness and infliction of emotional distress, all because she found a little extra in the bag of almonds that she purchased. That something extra was the infamous saw-toothed grain beetle.

Paulson's attorney says that the minute insect eventually took over the whole house. The infestation was so traumatic that the entire family eventually had to seek psychological counseling.

Some folks might think that it's a sport, but Robert Milarski, better known as Brother Igor, knows that professional wrestling is an art. And like any artist, he doesn't like it when attorneys and agents try to tell him how to practice his art. A performance suit brought by a promoter claimed that Milarski was cheating audiences of entertainment because he was ending his matches too soon. An attorney for the promoter admitted that they wanted to be able to tell Brother Igor what to do and how long to wrestle. "You have fifteen minutes to fill," he said. "We want you to use your fifteen minutes."

Kenneth M. Steinberg, Brother Igor's lawyer, saw the suit as cutting to the heart of one of the major philosophical questions facing us today: is professional wrestling a sport or entertainment? His warning was perfectly clear: "Wrestling entertainment as we know it may be invalid under state law."

I t took the Yellow Balloon hair salon of Los Angeles 13 minutes to cut a young boy's hair but only 10 minutes to cut a girl's. At the same, time they charged $12 for the girl's cut but only $10 for the boy's. That was enough to prompt Joni Zuckerbrow-Miller to sue for damages and file for an injunction to try to correct this social and economic miscarriage of justice.

Prior to any settlement, the Yellow Balloon did move to change it's pricing policy. They started to charge $11 for boys and $13 for girls.

R oy Rogers and Dale Evans filed a suit against the Happy Trails novelty and gift shop chain because they claim that the store chain misused and abused the well-known theme song of the celebrity couple. The lawsuit also claims that the stores sell drug paraphernalia. Not so, assured one store clerk who said, "Everything we sell is for tobacco."

Roy and Dale said that the use of the Happy Trails name ran counter to their "positive images as concerned, caring individuals and of champions of decency, law and justice."

069 perfectly expressed Michael Herbert Dengler's relationship with the universe, so he sued to have it become his legal name. One Zero, as he is known to his friends, ran into a legal roadblock when the County Attorney David Mikkel protested the move on the grounds that using a number for a name ran contrary to public policy.

Thwarted in his first attempt, Dengler then offered to settle for a change to Michael 10 Holtz. The Minnesota court nixed that suit as well.

rederick Koch (pronounced with a *'ch'*) of Vermont grew tired of having folks pronounce his name with a 'ke' on the end like the famous soft drink, so he sued to have his name legally changed to Frederick Coke-is-it. (It appears that the courts are a bit more creative in Vermont than in Minnesota). Our story, however, starts, rather than ends there. The Coca-Cola Company, yes, *that* Coca-Cola Company, sued Mr. Coke-is-it on the grounds that he might have changed his name in order to infringe on their rights.

Mr. Coke-is-it's attorney said that his client "wanted to make a statement about the little man vis-a-vis the large corporation." They settled out of court with Mr. Coke-is-it keeping his new name.

And if that wasn't enough, Coca-Cola had to contend with the announcement of Seattle public relations pro, Gary Mullins, that he was planning a class action suit to force Coca-Cola to deep six the "New Coke" and bring back the original recipe.

Mullins, founder of Old Cola Drinkers of America, Inc. said that the change to the "New Coke" formula had caused pain and suffering as well as run contrary to the constitutional rights of cola drinkers everywhere.

Darryl Ray Craig, a 17-year old from Beaumont, Texas, sued a Texas state trooper for $750,000, claiming that the trooper had interfered with Darryl Ray's religious freedom and had shown disregard for his health and safety. This all started when Darryl Ray drove his truck right into a utility pole on the way home from a rock concert.

According to Darryl Ray, trooper Douglas Fetters put him in the back of the patrol car and proceeded to give him a two-hour lecture during which he forced Darryl Ray to sign a pledge to dedicate his life to God and to list his sins.

The family court on Staten Island, New York convinced a judge to issue an order that prohibited two brothers, ages 13 and 16, from watching professional wrestling on television. The judge expressed concern that the mother had not taken steps to discourage the boys viewing regimen, particularly after the boys admitted that they got "hyped up" for hours after watching a match or when the 13-year old tried to get her in a "sleeper hold" while she was preparing dinner.

That's when mom admitted that she was a regular viewer, herself.

Attorney Patrick S. Moore sued newspaper columnist Ann Gerber for $300 million after she used the line, "There are no honest lawyers" three times in a single column. According to Moore, the columnist libeled the 30,000 attorneys residing in Cook County, Illinois.

Gerber's response was that she didn't mean to imply that all lawyers were dishonest, " just that all the honest ones were poor."

District Attorney Stephen Taylor of San Joaquin County, California brought a civil complaint against Arline Ek, HSG, and tried to fine her $50,000 for false advertising for running a mail order business that promised one-day Dominican Republic Divorces for $300 .

Ek asserted that she was qualified to be in the mail-order divorce business because she is a certified paralegal. Taylor denied that such an animal existed in California. When queried about what the HSG after her name stood for, Ek's response was that it stood for "high school graduate." "I just wanted initials behind my name," she said.

Sampson is a police dog. His owner and boss, the city of Casselbury, Florida, has been sued twice by individuals who claim that they have been bitten by Sampson. Two different insurance companies have refused to defend the suits, claiming that their coverage begins and ends with Sampson's work shift. The city disagreed, since Sampson, as all trained law enforcement officials, was on duty 24-hours a day. Now quit hanging around the water bowl and get back to work!

Computer manager and reformed alcoholic Wayne T. Hoover sued the Jack Daniels Distillery and the G. Heileman Brewing Company, claiming that they were negligent when they didn't clearly describe the dangers of drinking on the labels of their products. Cooper's suit contends that he suffered family conflicts, poor health, mood swings and couldn't hold a job as a result of his excessive tippling.

Cooper asked for $15,000 in damages and $4,800 to cover the costs of his rehabilitation, even though he admitted that he couldn't guarantee that he wouldn't have had a drink if there had been a warning on the label.

When company mechanics refused to respond to her request for assistance with a faulty windshield wiper, Chevron truck driver Barbara Reed parked her vehicle and went looking for a phone so she could call the highway patrol. On her way back to her rig she was knocked unconscious and raped by three men. She returned to work four days later. That's when Chevron announced that they were letting her go "for her own good." Suspecting that she just might be the victim of discrimination, Reed lodged a $5 million suit against Chevron.

Sherri "Sunshine" Hitterman knows what's in a name. She and six other hairstylists filed a suit against Fantastic Sam's, an international chain of beauty shops with facilities on three continents. The suit demanded that Fantastic Sam's abolish the practice of assigning cute nicknames like Bubbles, Peaches, Cookie and the aforementioned Sunshine to their

10,000 employees. Hair stylists who divulged their real names were threatened with dismissal.

Meyer Katsale swore that it happened like this: he took his first name, Meyer, and the first name of his partner, Jacob, and then changed that to Jacoby because that sounded better and then switched it around again and decided to call their Manhattan electronics store Jacoby and Meyers Electronics. That's how it happened. Honest.

Steven Meyers, founding partner of the franchise law firm Jacoby and Meyers, didn't buy it and brought a suit against the electronics firm claiming that they were "trying to pass themselves off as us." You could see how consumers would mistake the two, don't you?

Charles Marriner of Redding, Conecticut loved nature and in particular, he loved the ancient and venerable oak tree that graced his backyard. His neighbor, Arthur Anderson, loved television, his two-story high signal reception station and the Disney Channel. You can see where this one's going.

Anderson cut down the oak because it interfered with his ability to get the Disney Channel. Besides, he wasn't sure that the tree really was on Marriner's property. Marriner, on the other hand, was quite sure on whose property the tree was located and brought charges against his neighbor. At last report, he preferred staying out on his legal limb to Anderson's offer of $500 and free hauling of the dead tree if the suit were dropped.

Susan Ahlquist claimed that she was forced to quit her job because she refused to fetch coffee for Robert Abrahams, her boss, and wouldn't wash out his coffee cups. So she sued Abrahams for $2 million worth of sex discrimination. Abraham's response was that a man in his position" should not have to get his own coffee." He then indicated that his wife supported his position.

Arab was a real stud, professionally speaking, of course. It seems that on one excursion to Wales, he kind of 'pulled a muscle' after servicing 29 heifers on that single visit. That's when veterinarians told his owner, John Lloyd, that Arab needed rest and, most of all, abstinence if he was going to regain his professional standing. But it wasn't very long before Arab spied the bevy of bitchin' bovine babes one farm over, and quicker than you can say existential love god, he was over the fence and engaged in a night of dalliance that would end his stud bull days once and for all.

Lloyd sued his neighbor, Sara Ann Wright, for

$352,000, claiming that it was her cows that had damaged Arab's goods, as it were. The court disagreed and laid most of the blame on those 29 Welsh heifers. Lloyd was awarded $347.24. Arab will always have his memories.

A "man of the cloth" from Chicago clearly demonstrated the concept of lawsuit as cottage industry. In one four-year period he suffered two head injuries, six back injuries, two chest injuries, seven neck injuries and two injuries to his side. But that's not all. He also underwent 30 car accidents, four fires and a number of burglaries. Lucky for him he was only poisoned in a restaurant once. All that misfortune and he only retrieved a mere $100,000 for his troubles.

Imagine his shock and dismay when law enforcement officials implied that he might be engaged in insurance fraud. Why, the nerve.

And you thought that the revolution in Iran was tough on Jimmy Carter. Baron Enrico di Portanova sued ABC-TV for $20 million because the network broadcast a report that the Baron's mansion in Mexico was soon to house the deposed Shah of Iran. What upset the baron most of all was that the report was incorrect. It also meant that he and his wife would be considered enemies of the Ayatola.

The Baron claimed that he had never even been to Iran except for one quick stop to get some caviar.

Virginia Noland, a dental hygienist from Naperville, Illinois sued her employer, James LaRocco, claiming that LaRocco demanded that she and the other female workers in the office give him a goodbye hug each day as they left work. In the suit, Noland explained that she never would have taken the job if she had known that being both a hugger and a huggee were part of her professional duties. Noland also contended that LaRocco fired her because she tried to avoid his embrace. He said she quit.

Feminists take note. Mattel, Inc. considers Barbie to be more than just a pretty face. In fact, it considers her head to be intellectual -- property, that is. Mattel had Barbie's head protected by copyright in 1977, and used that as the basis for a suit against Kenner Products. Kenner was beginning to market a line of dolls based on the Miss America pageant that Mattel thought bore a wee bit too close a resemblance to Barbie.

Kenner fought back in the courtroom. They described in great detail the capital differences between their doll, Devon, and Mattel's Barbie. Devon, for instance, has a full chin and broader jaw ,while, at least according to Kenner, Barbie's short jaw protrudes "making her look as if she has an overbite...."

Canada has a little item they call the Family Law Reform Act, which states that upon reaching adulthood, a child has an obligation to help his or her parents financially. That made it possible for Paula Blum to sue her son Ephraim for support. Paula, 54, had been trying to get alimony from her ex-husband, but when that failed, she sued Ephraim, and the court ordered him to pay his mom $270 a month for the rest of her life and to cover her legal fees.

Paula wasn't done, however. At last report, she was trying to get the court to increase her stipend to a nice round figure; $2,000 a month.

Barbara Mossner's ex-husband placed a rather high value on his collection of posters and albums featuring the Chairman of the Board, one Francis Albert Sinatra. At least $80,000. And that's how much he sued his ex for when she customized the collection by adding a mustache and glasses to one poster in particular. "To be perfectly honest," she said, "Sinatra's never been one of my favorites."

The court apparently didn't share Mr. Mossner's opinion of Old Blue Eyes, either, and directed his ex to pay a settlement of $2,800.

Nancy Tattoli thought that the snail she ordered at the Limehouse restaurant might be a bit underdone, particularly when it walked off her plate. In her $350,000 suit against the restaurant she claimed that she was "disgusted and distressed" at the sight of the snail making its break for freedom. So much so, that when she tried to leave, she fell down the stairs and broke her ankle. The suit also contends that restaurant owner Kwang Jung told Ms. Tattoli that he would call the cops and called her a troublemaker when she indicated to him that someone in the kitchen had failed to slug the slug.

Carrie Millis used to baby sit for Edwin and Barbara Laupmanis. Used to is the key phrase here. They sued Ms. Millis for $10,000 in damages when they saw what was left of their house after returning from a weekend jaunt to Ohio. There was a fire still smoldering in the kitchen. Unfortunately, it wasn't in the stove or a fireplace. Their stereo was trashed, as was their chandelier. But at least those objects were still there. That's more than they could say for the raccoon coat, jewelry and coins that were just plain gone.

Ms. Millis, with an obvious gift for under-statement, described it all as "just a crazy weekend." The destruction apparently started when a simple invitation to her boyfriend turned into a full-blown party, and things went downhill from there. Millis conceded that she found the idea of a $10,000 law suit pretty daunting, admitting that she didn't even know how to go about finding an attorney. That should change pretty quickly.

Orlando Sentinel columnist Bob Morris thought he was being funny when he announced in his column that Pope John Paul II would make a guest appearance in a future episode of Miami Vice as a papal drug smuggler.

Mary Burns didn't think it was so funny. In fact she described it as "extremely vulgar" and sued the paper for $11 million. An action she says she took for herself and other "ordinary Catholics" injured by the remark.

I guess I'd better stick to medicine, because I sure don't understand the judicial system." Those words were uttered by Dr. Dudley O. Scott when a judge ordered that the good doctor was obligated to fulfil the conditions of a support agreement, despite the fact that his wife had hired two men to assault him.

According to the judge's ruling, Scott's wife and children had no other means of support, therefore Scott would have to continue to pay $1,500 per month until their divorce agreement became final. The judge's ruling did not indicate how the doctor would have fulfilled his financial obligation if the assault had been fatal.

Catholics aren't the only believers turning to the secular courts for justice. A number of folks who worship Pele, the Hawaiian volcano goddess, brought a suit against developers who wanted to declare a 9,000 acre area around the Kilauea Volcano a geothermal resource. Pele's worshipers said that the developers would desecrate the body of the goddess by digging around the volcano. The Hawaii Supreme Court decided to risk the wrath of the goddess and ruled in favor of the developers.

Marie Ezell admitted that she was feeling a bit lonely, so she asked if Margo Delores could spend some time with her. Harold Ezell said that that would be fine as long as Margo returned in time to participate in his granddaughter's slumber party. When Marie failed to bring Margo home on time, Harold sued her for $3,000 and custody of Margo. A court ruled that Margo did indeed belong with Harold but the judge thought that $3,000 was a bit excessive for a Cabbage Patch doll. He directed Marie to either return Margo or cough up $275 to Harold.

A jury in Nueces County, Texas ruled that the Brown-Forman Corporation was only 35 percent liable in the death of Marie Brinkmyer. That was enough, however, for the jury to award her mother $1.5 million in damages. Ms. Brinkmyer, an 18-year old college freshman, died after consuming 20 ounces of 80-proof tequila in a single night. James Ragan, the Brinkmeyer's attorney, successfully argued that the tequila was an unreasonably dangerous product and as such, Brown-Forman should have explicitly warned consumers about the danger that could result from overindulging.

The $1.5 million award will eventually be reduced by 65% before it is paid out. The 65% represents the late Ms. Brinkmeyer's percentage of neglect in the case.

Donald Tinker-Bey, a 'retired' burglar currently enjoying the hospitality of the state of Illinois in their facility at Marion, thought that prison officials had been less than dutiful when they lost his sweatshirts, tennis shoes and pajama bottoms while he was being transferred. He sued prison officials for $150.00.

Not a large sum, but certainly larger than the $10.00 settlement accepted by one inmate who had sued the prison over the loss of cardboard file folder, four shoelaces and a jar of cream (previously opened).

Traveling faith-healers Charles and Frances Hunter held something they called a "Healing Explosion" at their City of Light Ministry. Evelyn Kuykendall attended the faith healing in order find some relief from her constant back pain, but things didn't go quite as planned. It was during the "Healing Explosion" that Kuykendall fell and fractured her back.

She subsequently sued the Hunters, even though they argued that she "fell in a peculiar way" and the burden for the injury was on God. A jury, however, disagreed with the Hunters and placed the burden for the injury squarely on them, to the tune of $300,000.

"If the town of Rutherford is stupid enough to spend money on this case, I will continue it."

We don't always get what we order, whether we're in a restaurant or a hospital. Consider the woman in California who suffered irreparable damage to her lungs because of an improperly administered enema. The court did, and ordered the hospital to pay a judgment of $250,000.

Attorney William Sheffield ordered a St. Bernard puppy from a monastery in Switzerland. He even paid the deposit. Sorry to say, the pup didn't survive the journey to Sheffield's home in California, and when the monks refused to return his deposit, he decided to sue. But Sheffield didn't mess around with the monastery. He went after the home office, suing the

Vatican for $400 for breach of contract.

Sheffield won the suit. Collecting on it, however, has been another matter. The Pope or Vatican officials have yet to pay the $400. Perhaps he should request that they take up a special collection this Sunday.

A judge in Los Angeles, California had good news for attorney Herb Blitz. It's just a shame he couldn't hear it. Herb's ex-wife had gone to court to argue that just because he was in a coma, she didn't think that that was enough of a reason to excuse him from his alimony payments. What with his heart still pumping and his lungs still moving and all, it was obvious that he was still alive.

The court thought otherwise and freed the comatose Blitz from his alimony obligation, at least while he was in the coma.

Randall Dale Adams was languishing in prison when film producer Errol Morris became interested in his story. Adams had been convicted of murder, but Morris believed him to be innocent and proceeded to make a film, *The Thin Blue Line*, about Adams' case. In addition to winning awards, the movie's reassessment of the evidence of the case and the prosecutor's actions was so compelling that a state appeals court threw out Randall Dale Adams' conviction for murder.

While Adams appreciated Morris's efforts on his behalf, he will be the first to tell you that business is business. That's why he decided to sue Morris to regain control of the rights to his life story. Adams contended that Morris lost control of the rights when Morris failed to exercise a two-year option on the story, which would have cost him $10.00.

Some folks have unique ways of cooperating with one another. After several attempts to get her boss to kick the tobacco habit, Claudia Marshall left a rather polite note that asked her boss to consider the impact of her habit on the workplace and asked her to stop smoking . She closed the note by thanking her boss for her cooperation. Within 30 minutes Marshall's boss cooperated by firing her. Marshall cooperated right back by filing a $100,000 law suit for back pay and punitive damages. The suit was the first of its kind under San Francisco's anti-smoking ordinance.

In the mid-80's, a number of Florida law firms engaged in the practice of adding words and names that begin with the letter A to the beginning of the name of the firm, in an effort to get a competitive advantage in the way that they were listed in the phone book. In 1989, the Florida Supreme Court ordered that the practice was permissible as long as the firm used that name on everything else: letterheads, court documents.... everything.

Now you may find this difficult to believe, but as a result of the ruling most firms have gone back to their real names.

The Bastrop, Texas school district segregated 8-year old Zacharia Toungate in a private classroom because they thought that his 7-inch ponytail violated the school dress code. Zach's parents didn't see it that way, and sued to have him returned to the general population on the grounds that the ruling was unconstitutional, since it didn't apply to girls as well.

When Wendy Jean Allredge was divorced in 1988, she asked the Utah Driver License Division to reissue her a license with her maiden name instead of her former husband's last name. The Division said that it would be glad to do it providing she got her ex-husband's permission. She pointed out that she had already changed her name on Social Security, tax and bank records with no problem. Her attorney pointed out that when a woman gets married in Utah she can easily change her name on the license without her husband's permission. The Driver License Division still refused to budge, claiming that the policy helped to guard against fraud. Allredge sued in federal court. She lost the case.

Probate judge Felix Felton of Tuscumbia, Alabama thought that he was doing the Lord's will when he refused to issue a marriage license to Edward Sharpley and Tahlia Odom. Sharpley is black and Odom is white. They sued in federal court, which found Judge Felton in violation of the federal law outlawing state miscegenation laws.

Over the course of several months Louise O'Boyle made a number of visits to Mary Lynn, a free-lance psychic, in order to remove a curse that had followed her late husband into the afterworld. It seemed that in addition to providing spiritual counsel, Mary Lynn was adept at divining the depth of Mrs. O'Boyle's financial resources. O'Boyle ended up paying over $9,000 for the psychic services.

Lynn must have had *some* psychic abilities because she left town just before O'Boyle sued her for fraud.

The ACLU sued to have the Adolescent Family Life Act, a federal law that encourages teenage chastity, declared unconstitutional on the grounds that a number of religious groups were using federal funds to promote some rather extreme interpretations of both the law and scripture.

Attorney Janet Benshoof presented the example

of one group that suggested that young women could suppress their carnal urges by pretending that Jesus was their date.

Joey Coyle must have thought that he had hit the jackpot on God's own slot machine the day he saw $1.2 million drop from the back of a Purolator armored car. Coyle scooped up the booty and went on a spree that saw him spend $196,000 in six days. He was arrested when he tried to leave the country.

Even though Coyle was acquitted of theft charges by reason of insanity, he felt that the incident had changed his life forever. So he did what any sane, insane man would do. He sued the Purolater company, claiming that their negligence had started his slide down that slippery slope. A movied deal ensued, followed by...well, we don't want to give away the ending.

Judge Michael Nolan of London, England ruled that the Costello family of Nottingham did indeed have the right to sue the Nottingham City Council for failing to provide them with ghost-free subsidized housing. The city council had ruled that the Costellos did not qualify for government housing because they had chosen of their own free will to leave their home.

The Costellos had left their house after witnessing a series of events that included lights turning on in the night, moving bed clothes, shattered windows and holy water being spit back into the face of a priest who had tried to exorcise the poltergeists.

A 25-year old Chicago woman, identified in court documents as 'Jane Doe,' sued American Airlines for $12 million, alleging that an employee of the airline prevented her from boarding a plane and, after an argument, bit Ms. Doe on the ring and index finger. The employee eventually underwent a series of test that indicated that he had been exposed to the AIDS virus. American Airlines claims that their employee acted in self defense.

Bill Webb, teacher and part time fashion plate, was suspended and eventually fired by the Madison County, West Virginia Board of Education for breaching its faculty dress code. His infraction? Not wearing a tie. A math teacher for 19 years, Webb sued to get his job back and the court agreed with him, ruling that he had been wrongfully dismissed because the dress code had been improperly imposed.

Fine, said the Board of Education, and announced that they were rewriting the dress code. Only this time, they were going to ban clothes made of denim as well. That might be too much for Webb who vowed not to return if there is a prohibition against denim.

In 1980, Jane Messina of Boston, Massachusettes brought a law suit seeking triple damages from Debbie's Pet Land because Sheba, the sulfur-crested cockatoo that she purchased from Debbie's in 1978, had yet to speak. After listening to a veterinarian who testified that not all cockatoos speak, the judge dismissed the suit . As the judge put it, "Some are smarter than others; some are retards."

Often, it's the little things that you notice first when a relationship goes bad. That's what happened with Kinky. Kinky's owner got suspicious when the dog started staying out late night after night. He finally sued his neighbor for enticing Kinky to leave home by feeding the dog. A British judge agreed that the neighbor had broken up a previously happy home and issued an injunction that prevented the neighbor from seeing and feeding Kinky on a regular basis.

Paula Makopoulous of Morristown, New Jersey sued Disney World for $6 million, contending that her four-year-old son experienced psychological trauma when they visited the Florida branch of the Magic Kingdom in 1983. Makopoulous claims that when her son, Evan, grabbed the tail of Mickey Mouse, an "apparently intoxicated person in a mouse suit" grabbed her son and tossed him against a railing, causing the alleged trauma. According to his mom, Evan eventually required more than $10,000 in therapy because he had believed in Mickey Mouse before the incident.

Oscar Nichols was serving time at the federal facility at Lexington, Kentucky on a gun charge. Weighing in at a rather svelte 600 pounds, he came to be of the opinion that prisons are designed for thin people, which to him smacked of discrimination. Nichols filed a $30 million suit in which he contended that he would never make it out alive if he didn't get the essentials like an air-conditioned room and housekeeping assistance.

Some people will risk their all for justice. Consider the Ohio inmate serving a sentence of 4 to 25 years. He typed his appeal on toilet paper. In closing, he said, "If I get another illiterate, biased and prejudiced decision from this court before my next issue of paper, I'm going to be hurting."

It didn't take Polish graphic designer Zbignew Karkuszewski long to get into the swing of things on his trip to the U.S. He sued his in-laws for $200,000, claiming that they were negligent in letting their cockatiel fly around the house.

In a series of events that would have done Rube Goldberg proud, the bird perched on the wine rack, knocking loose a bottle of wine which fell on Ziggy's left foot, severing a tendon and causing $200,000 worth of permanent disfigurement, according to the lawsuit.

Palm Beach, Florida attorney Allen DeWeese sued the town and town officials over its ordinance that outlaws shirtless jogging. The ordinance calls for anyone 14 or older to keep the upper part of their body covered when in public. DeWeese thinks the ordinance is unconstitutional. "I personally think that leisure suits on men and short shorts on elderly, overweight, geriatric women are far more offensive," he said. DeWeese has been charged with "indecent exposure-lewdness" for violating the ordinance.

Remember the old TV commercial that posed the eternal question about prunes? Are five enough? Are six too many? The same kind of question apparently applies to baking soda as well, and Timothy Smith asked a San Francisco court to answer it. Smith admitted to having had a little heartburn and turning to baking soda in order to relieve his gastric distress. That's when, as he put it, his stomach exploded. Smith brought a product liability action against the makers of Arm & Hammer Baking Soda.

A young woman in Arkansas was quite disgusted when she saw the condition of the public toilet that she needed to use. Not finding any paper to cover the seat, she tried to use the facility by standing on the seat. Of course, she slipped and fell. Of course, she sued.

The Arkansas Supreme Court dismissed the claim with the observation that the seat just wasn't designed to be used that way.

In addition to a full tank and a good deal on mileage, car rental companies are now obligated to tell folks where to go and where not to go. That's the premise of a suit brought by the families of German tourists killed by robbers in Florida. They have sued the Alamo Rent A Car Co. in Dade County court on the grounds that the company was negligent when it failed to warn foreign visitors to avoid high-crime areas.

Ian Berg is a young man with lofty aspirations. Berg, 16, wanted to run for the post of district justice in Montgomery County, PA. In order to do so, he had to bring a suit against the Montgomery County Board of Elections that argued that just because he didn't belong to a political party and wasn't old enough to register to vote, he still had a right to run.

The state Supreme Court agreed with Berg and

ruled that he could run. They were quick to point out, however, that the ruling did not mean that if elected he could serve. That could take a separate ruling. The justices weren't sure that Berg could carry out the duties of the office without breaking the child labor laws.

A woman from Hamburg, Germany brought what could be called an aesthetic action against a woman with whom she shared a communal garden. The plaintiff argued that the other woman had inserted two little decorative gnomes in the garden. The plaintiff found the gnomes to be "symbols of narrow mindedness and stupidity" and "offended her aesthetic sense," so of course, she sued. The court ruled that the gnomes were not "aesthetic" and ordered them removed at once.

Back when he was a State Senator for Colorado, Tim Wirth had to file an action against one of his constituents just to get a little peace and quiet. Diane Frances Doster had spared nothing in her efforts to make Wirth aware of the special relationship that she knew existed between them: a bond of ESP and romance. Finally, Doster was arrested when she took an apartment that was located just steps away from Wirth's office, violating a permanent restraining order that forbad her to come within two blocks of the Senator's home or place of business.

When the court refused to release Doster until she could prove that she had found another apartment, she made it clear that mere miles couldn't keep her separated from her true love. She admitted that she could keep tabs on Wirth by using ESP to communicate with the family dog.

Just in case you needed more evidence that times have changed, the Los Angeles District Attorney's Office, a bold and brazen article if there ever was one, filed child abuse charges against a Roman Catholic nun who was teaching in a Los Angeles, California Catholic grammar school.

The suit alleges that the nun threw a 9-year-old girl against a wall and attempted to motivate an 8-year-old boy by lifting him off the ground by his cheeks, punching him, stepping on his foot and rapping him across the knuckles with a ruler.

A customer returned a hand gun that he had purchased in a department store in the San Fernando Valley, California. His complaint was that the safety didn't work. The store clerk was sure that that couldn't be the case so he picked up the gun and pulled the trigger. What do you know? The customer was right.

When the gun discharged, the bullet pierced the clerk's palm and proceeded on to the Music Department, where it penetrated the left arm of Marc J. Katzman, landscape gardener and plaintiff. Katzman settled out of court for $100,000.

There is no bond closer than the one between a man and his pig. Consider Nick DiGiaimo and his miniature pig, Fideau. DiGiamo went to court to appeal the Rutherford, New Jersey ordinance that makes it illegal to keep a pig in the house, but not before he and his swine took it on the lam to upstate New York.

"If the town of Rutherford is stupid enough to spend money on this case," he said, "I will continue it."

An Ellet, Ohio woman sued Wonder Bread on the grounds that it did more than build strong bodies twelve ways. She says that it also left the body parts lying around. Shirley Collins contends that she was putting several slices of bread in her toaster when she noticed that a human finger was imbedded in one of them .

Collin's suit says that, because of the foreign substance that she found in the slice, she underwent emotional distress, physical injury and incurred medical costs with more to come in the future. The suit did not request a specific amount of damages. In a side note, the local coroner's office said that it didn't have a comment on the case because they only get involved in cases concerning whole bodies.

Kisha Jamerson, a cat also known as 'the plaintiff,' was so excited about having her new toy that she swallowed it, complete with bell and string. That necessitated emergency surgery to remove the toy, which came to $643. But her pain and suffering didn't end there. Kisha's owner, Sonia Jamerson, said that Kisha is now frightened by bells and is afraid to play.

So Sonia sued the company that made the toy, Vo-Toys, and the place where she purchased it, Petco, on the grounds that the toy wasn't a suitable thing for a cat to play with in the first place, even with the bell and the string. She settled out of court for $400.

The Missouri Attorney General's Office knew that it had a problem on its hands when it received close to twenty complaints about Joseph Barr, talent scout and barber. That's when they issued an injunction against him, and began preparing a criminal suit alleging fraud. It seems that Barr had invited a number of hopeful actors in the St. Louis area to his hotel room which doubled as his barber shop. He then offered them a chance to land a part in a commercial for the U.S

Army. The prospective stars were to get $200 up front and $16,000 once the shoot was done.

The only hitch was that they had to sport a military style haircut. That wasn't much of a problem, though, because Barr was only too glad to give them a crew cut on the spot for free. As surprising as it may seem, Barr wasn't really an agent and there wasn't any commercial.

Builder Barry Larson wanted to sue his neighbor, Mike Waldrop, but found that there weren't any laws that covered Mike's artwork: a drawing of a man dropping his pants and exposing his backside. This was no sketch. The drawing was 7-feet tall and faced a lot where Larson was building a house. He claimed that Waldrop drew the portrait in order to make it difficult for him to sell the house. The local DA told him that while that may be true, it didn't violate any laws, since Oak Grove, Oregon didn't have an ordinance against ugly.

A London woman sued her husband for divorce on the grounds that he was cheap, and she seemed to have ample evidence. He charged his wife for painting the living room ceiling and charged his daughter when she used the shower. He even charged the family to cover the electricity they used when watching the television. After 36 years of marriage, the thrifty bricklayer refused to even consider taking his wife on a belated honeymoon because he thought the cost to be prohibitive. The divorce was granted.

John Ted Wright filed an appeal to have his conviction on a rape charges thrown out on the grounds that he was denied the opportunity to introduce evidence that he thinks would have proven his innocence: his penis. Wright claimed that he was so well endowed that he could have not been involved, since the facts of the case pointed toward an individual of more modest physical means. The judge in the case refused Wright's offer to provide the jury with a photo of his alibi, a wooden model or, failing all else, to display himself to the jury. Appeal denied.

Not all appeal actions are dismissed. Jon Clifford Johnson won his suit before the Minnesota Court of Appeals. Police had stopped Johnson at 1a.m. while he was on his way home and asked to see his driver's license. Johnson admitted that he didn't have it on him and told the police officers that he was headed home to get it. That's when he took off at the breakneck speed of 15 mph. Johnson was coming home from planting his soybean fields and was driving his pickup truck. If that wasn't enough, this reckless speed merchant was towing a trailer.

Police officer Ronald Morris not only gave chase, he radioed ahead for a roadblock. It was there where police finally stopped Johnson by shooting out his tires. A lower court convicted Johnson of fleeing an officer. That was thrown out by the appeal court, which said that the whole adventure really wasn't necessary, and if officer Morris had wanted to write Johnson a ticket he knew where he lived.

Gerald Mayo was well aware that Satan had made his life miserable numerous times and had prepared the way for his downfall, so he sued the Angel of Death in federal court on a civil rights violation. The suit, *Gerald Mayo v. Satan & his staff,* was dismissed because the court doubted that Mayo could actually get personal jurisdiction over the defendant. The court was also concerned that once word of the law suit was made public it would become a class action suit.

The Miller Brewing Co. wanted to buy the folks up in Wisconsin a cold one, but first they had to go to court to do it. In an action brought in Dane County court, Miller asked to have the practice of "trade spending" declared legal. The law against having brewers give tavern owners or their patrons "something of value" dates back to the repeal of prohibition and makes it illegal for a salesman from Miller or any other brewery to walk into a tavern and buy a round for the bar or even one drink for an individual.

Miller claimed that buying a beverage for patrons was a form of advertising and as such, it was protected by the First Amendment.

Byron De La Beckwith's attorney entered a motion before the Mississippi Supreme Court which claimed murder charges against his client should be dismissed because the aging segregationist couldn't get a fair trial. Beckwith was charged for the third time with the shooting death of civil rights worker Medgar Evers.

Beckwith's attorney claimed that too much time had passed since the crime for his client to get a fair trial. Two previous trials on the same charge have ended in mistrials.

In an attempt to prevent the Little Rock schools from sponsoring activities that celebrated Halloween, an Arkanasas attorney filed a suit that included the following in the list of defendants: the Department of Education, the school district, the school board, the High Priests of Secular Humanism, the Communist Party of the USA, the Church of Satan, the Anti-Christ and last but not least, Satan, the God of This World System.

Satan did not go undefended. Attorney John Wesley Hall signed on as the devil's counsel and argued that the suit was without standing and should be dismissed because the plaintiff failed to prove that Satan either owned property or wrote contracts in the state.

A Montana pig farmer sued the state and was awarded $240,000 after claiming that the construction of a new state highway was stressful to his pigs. The key testimony in the case was provided by veterinarian Earl Pruyn, of Missoula, who described the nature of "porcine stress syndrome" to the jury.

Doris Barnett won $100 in the California state lottery. She should have quit while she was ahead. That $100 prize entitled her to spin a roulette wheel with a chance to win even more cash. When the ball came to a stop on the wheel, it indicated that she was a $3 million winner. Barnett, described by her attorney as a very large woman, began to hop around. While she hopped, lights flashed, balloons floated by, and the ball fell from the $3 million perch to the $10,000 perch. When last heard from, Doris was preparing her suit against the California Lottery Commission in an effort to get her millions back.

An Orange County, California woman fought the ticket that she received for driving alone in the car pool lane by arguing that since she was pregnant she was wasn't really alone. The court ruling on her appeal was that for the purposes of forming a two-person car pool, an unborn child was indeed a person.

A woman sued the Greyhound bus company and was awarded $4,300 for damages resulting from emotional distress. The distress was caused by having the bus swerve while she was in the bathroom of the bus, causing her buttocks to become lodged in the bus window.

A funeral home located in Abilene, Texas sued the local telephone company for $300,000 for listing their ad in the wrong section of the Yellow Pages, the frozen food section. The funeral home alleged that it was held up to ridicule and was receiving crank calls inquiring about what kind of meat was on sale.

When workers at a Vallejo, California cemetery saw that the grave was not large enough to accommodate the coffin intended for it, they tried to slide the coffin in by turning it on its side. When that

didn't work they tried taking the handles off. And when
that didn't work they tried to force it in the grave by
jumping up and down on the lid, breaking the coffin in
two. That was enough for the family of the deceased,
who sued the cemetery for $500,000.

Velna Turnage attended a performance of the
Christy Brothers Circus as a guest of the owners.
Ms. Turnage was sitting in the front row, when one
of the trained dancing horses backed toward her and
deposited a very special and warm personal memento of
the performance right in her lap. She sued the circus for
$500 in damages for mental suffering, humiliation and
embarrassment.

"O God, please let me get away with it just this once."

A California woman was injured on one of the state's many highways when a piece of a brake drum flew off of a passing truck and crashed through her windshield. In a demonstration of that special kind of legal logic that only makes sense to folks on the left-hand coast, she sued the state. She claimed that the Highway Patrol officers who stopped to help her actually destroyed her chances of suing the truck driver because they failed to pursue the truck. Have a nice day.

Dallas, Texas resident Jimmy W. Janacek sued Triton Energy Corp. because he thought that he had been unjustly fired when he challenged other corporate executives to release negative financial information to shareholders. A Dallas jury agreed and awarded Janacek $124 million -- the largest award for damages in the history of a state known for doing things on a big scale. Juror Gayla Bruner said "We wanted to say something to large corporations that might think they are above being dealt with." Ms. Bruner also saw the irony in the fact that the decision was handed down by a group of jurors making "six bucks a day."

Now, you might have heard about the battling Davises. You know, the couple that filed for divorce two months after fertilizing nine eggs that had been removed from Mrs. Davis' ovaries. Seven of these eggs, now called pre-embryos by the courts, were frozen, to be used at a later time. You might have even heard that Mrs. Davis' ex, Junior, sued to gain legal control of the pre-embryos in order to prevent them from being fertilized, and that the court ruled that Junior Davis had "a constitutionally protected right not to beget a child where no pregnancy has taken place."

What you probably didn't realize was that Junior's professional training made him the perfect man to bring this suit: he's a refrigeration technician.

Substitute teacher Dietrich Katterman sued the Randolph New Jersey School system for violating his constitutional right to free speech when they fired him for comparing the Boy Scouts to the Hitler

Youth. The school district said that his comments had been considered offensive by some students. The German-born Katterman, who joined the Hitler Youth at age 10 said, "I was stating the facts as I knew them...I enjoyed it, my brothers did and my sisters did....They had activities that kids enjoy -- camping, singing, crafts. We made presents for underprivileged kids at Christmas."

In an example of what happens when you have a light judicial calendar, Judge Jack Carl of Alabama issued a directive from the bench that ordered the University of Alabama at Birmingham basketball team to beat the University of Virginia in the NCAA Mideast Regional Tournament. The judge also directed students, citizens and fans to root for Alabama. The judge served the papers himself.

The lawyers at Universal Studios made it clear to Professor Albert E. Millar of Christopher Newport College that they were not to be trifled with. They let it be known that they were revving up their law suit machine and were prepared to unleash it if MIllar didn't stop distributing his four-page pamphlet that discussed the things that Jesus and the movie character E.T. had in common. If he continued to infringe on their copyright he would reap the whirlwind. Or words to that effect.

An associate judge in Chicago, Illinois was indicted for his attempt to streamline the criminal justice system. Paul T. Foxgrover told at least 21 defendants that they should pay their fines directly to him.

Foxgrover's attempts at judicial innovation netted him $16,000 in a single year. It also netted him 86 felony counts.

Attorney Ray Newman submitted a bill to Los Angeles County for 25 hours of legal work that was performed over a particular weekend. He must have misplaced his calendar, because he seems to have forgotten that it was the same weekend that he was in jail on a drunk-driving charge.

Newman was indicted on five counts of grand larceny and perjury as a result of over billing the county to the tune of $1.3 million over a three-year period. Newman asked to be represented by a public defender because he couldn't afford a lawyer.

The South Carolina Supreme Court ruled that because attorney Gabrielle Eliot had never passed go she couldn't collect the $200. Despite being a high school drop out and never attending college, Eliot became an attorney and went on to earn a master's degree. That didn't cut any ice with the court, who disbarred her because she didn't have a high school or a college degree.

Not only did he see him, but the policeman also heard Morris Davie as plain as day. Davie was on his knees, with his hands raised and praying, "O God, please let me get away with it just this once." In Davie's first trial for setting a forest fire, his attorneys successfully argued that prayer was privileged communication and thus couldn't be entered into evidence. An appeals court disagreed, however, ruling that private communication existed only between human beings and that did not apply to God. They ordered a new trial which included the prayer as evidence.

If you ever go camping with Robert Eugene Low, make sure you keep the coughdrops away from him. His friend didn't, and so he had to sue Low for $1.5 million. While on a camping trip, Low consumed over 100 boxes of cough suppressants. He then began to rant and rave about religion and Satan, stabbed his friend in the back and torched the tent. Low's attorney argued successfully that the combination of the cough drops and the thin mountain air produced Low's aggressive state of mind. The judge believed him and ruled that when Low was on his coughdrop jag he lacked the presence of mind necessary to meet the legal definition of assault. The state is appealing the dismissal, and the friend is still suing.

At age 17, Steve Baccus was thought to be the youngest practicing attorney in the U.S. Despite being a member of the Florida bar, the New York State courts ruled that he couldn't sit for their bar exam because their minimum age is 21. In response to the ruling, Mr. Baccus, Esq. announced that he would file an age discrimination suit and then return home to Miami where he intended to establish a law firm.

Residents of Warren, Ohio went to court to get Ronald Testa to remove his three-year-old lion cub, Wally, from the neighborhood. Testa successfully fought the first round of the legal battle by arguing that Wally had never seen another lion cub and, consequently, didn't even know that he was one. The case went to appeal.

The New Hampshire Civil Liberties Union sued to have the Milford city council change its policy of refusing to let local children collect money for UNICEF at Halloween. The ACLU folks argued that the ban violates First Amendment rights. "We have a very conservative town here, and some people just don't like the United Nations," said a local minister. Several city council members charged that UNICEF funnels money to communist governments.

Jeanne O'Kon called Jim Smith's bluff. A bar owner in Tallahassee, Smith had offered $25 to anyone sporting a T-shirt with a date on it prior to 1977. He also offered to pay an extra $5 for each additional year before 1976. O'Kon sauntered into Smith's bar with a T-shirt commemorating the 900th anniversary of the erection of the Tower of London in 1078. Smith balked at paying and O'Kon sued. When the jury awarded her the entire $4,490 Smith response was, "Thank God she didn't visit the Sphinx or something."

James and Mary D'Orio didn't think it was right for their daughter, Allison, to be suspended just because she ditched a class trip while in New York. They made their point by hiring Tickles the Clown to show up at Allison's 8th grade graduation. Tickles serenaded the school's dean, handed him a bouquet of balloons and hit him in the face with a cream pie. Tickles admitted to the police that the D'Orios hired him and paid him $10,000 not to mention their name, which he did the first chance he got.

While the dean was preparing his civil suit, the D'Orios were charged with tampering and attempting to bribe a witness. Mrs. D'Orio eventually got 30 days in jail and a $1,000 fine. Tickles the Clown walked on all charges.

Barbara McCann had been a juror for 621 days. That's more than one-and-a-half years. She had listened to 182 witnesses and examined over 6,000 exhibits and pieces of evidence in a very complex personal injury lawsuit in which 65 plaintiffs sought $135 million in damages from the Monsanto Company.

McCann was dismissed from the jury 30 minutes before deliberations began because one of the attorneys for the plaintiff was involved in a suit against her relatives. "I would have liked to voice my opinion," she said.

Then there is the case of the Australian who was saved by the size of the stash and his briefs -- the non-legal kind. Andrews Salvador was convicted in an Indian court of smuggling hashish in his underwear and was sentenced to ten years in jail and a fine of $28,000. He won his appeal by demonstrating to the court that the briefs entered into evidence in his first trial were too small to be his and certainly too small to accommodate both him and the block of hash.

In another case involving those no-pain Dominican divorces, The Wisconsin Supreme Court ruled that the 1,200 Dominican divorces that attorney Davis Donnelly had sold to his clients were not recognized in the state. The court ordered him to contact each client individually and inform them that they are still married. When asked how he could sell divorces that he knew were worthless to his clients, he reportedly replied that he did "not inquire or clutter his mind about the law."

Officers from the Municipal Council and Religious Department in Kota Baru, Malaysia raided the Buluh Kuba Bazaar after receiving a tip that patrons there might be "behaving in an improper manner." They brought criminal charges against two men and two women on the grounds that they were suspected of dancing.

Richard Richards brought an action against the state of Missouri, claiming that he should be released from the State's Training Center for Men where he is serving a life sentence because, as far as he can tell, he has fulfilled the terms of his sentence. Richards underwent surgery to have a pacemaker implanted in his heart, during which his heart stopped for two-and-a-half minutes. As far as Richards is concerned, that marks the end of his natural life and thus the completion of his sentence. He is also seeking damages for each day in prison after the operation.

In order to prepare for the Illinois Bar exam, a number of recent law school graduates checked into hotels that were located near the site of the exam. They thought that they would at least get some peace and quiet and a good night's sleep. What they got instead was a road construction crew that went on all through the night. One of the barristers-to-be tried his wings by going to court and seeking an injunction to shut down the construction. Motion denied.

Beekeeper Lee Pongi claimed that his bees were frightened away by the constant sound of artillery fire that came from a nearby army base. He sued the Korean government and was awarded $1,500 in damages.

Sister Candida, President of Rosary College, was quite surprised when she saw her photo gracing a greeting card that said "It's all right for you to kiss me." On the inside the punch line read " So long as you don't get in the habit." Beside it being an old joke, she didn't think that it was all that funny, so she went to court and got an injunction that forbad the card's manufacturer, California Dreamers, Inc., from distributing the card. The company's president said that they didn't realize that the person in the photo was actually a nun. "If it was a model that was used, it's a funny card. But it's not funny if it's a real nun."

A Capitol Hill business person brought a suit against Ellen Proxmire, wife of former Senator William Proxmire, on the grounds that her status as a senator's wife gave her an unfair business advantage.

Nope, said the Federal Appeals court which ruled, "simple use of one's status in society is not itself illegal."

California Superior Court Judge Charles McGrath demonstrated that seeing isn't always believing in an arson case that revolved around a flare, a portable toilet and that scourge of the modern world, a video tape. Three young men had videotaped themselves while they dropped a lighted flare in a portable toilet. They also ran the tape while they broke into a parking area and set off fire alarms. The trio even recorded firefighters response to the blazing toilet.

That still wasn't enough for McGrath, who

acquitted the trio on the grounds that the tape did not prove that they had intended to start a fire when they dropped the flare. "...there's nothing obvious to me that dropping a flare down a toilet is going to start a fire," said the judge.

In another example of efforts to bring a touch of romance into the courtroom, a San Francisco CPA went to court to recover costs and damages from a young lady who stood him up on a date. The court ruled that he did not have a case but it did order that a torn, red cardboard heart that the CPA had entered into evidence as being symbolic of his feelings should be returned to him.

The Very Important Day Care and Preschool thought that the mural that depicted a number of Disney characters would be a nice touch. The Disney attorneys didn't agree, and informed the school that the mural implied that the Disney corporation had given its seal of approval to the 90-student school. Disney warned that they had begun to take legal action to force the school to remove the murals. Perhaps the most important argument in this case has already been cast by a student. "If they try to take them down I'll cry," said 8-year-old Kristina Pulido. Which explains why some people go into law and some people go into marketing.

In a case that won't remind anyone of Ferante and Teicher, heart specialist Dr. Newton Friedman went to court to secure visitation rights that enabled him to return each week to the home that he had shared with his estranged wife. The objects of his affection were the couple's two pianos -- a $12,000 Steinway and a $28,000 Bösendorfer. His wife complied with the ruling at first, but eventually changed the doorlocks, claiming that his regular visits to tickle the ivories was an invasion of her privacy.

So they went back to court and arrived at another solution for managing their discontent duet: Howard got the Bösendorfer and wife Carol got the Steinway.

The U.S. Navy know negligence when they see it. That's why they brought a summary court martial against Hospital Corpsman 3rd Class James Ashley for sewing the ear of an inebriated sailor to a table while treating him in a navy clinic in Virginia Beach. Ashley was fined $200 and had his rank reduced from E4 to E3. One can only wonder if he sewed the new stripes on his uniform himself.

The Speedo 690 restaurant was located on the former site of an auto parts store of the same name. The owners of the beach-theme restaurant liked the name and kept it. That didn't present a problem for the former owners of the store, but it did raise the hackles of the Speedo swimsuit company. They sued, claiming that diners are likely to confuse the food served by the restaurant with the snug spandex suits manufactured by the company.

Everyone has a few skeletons in his closet, but the officials of an elementary school near Chicago got tired of finding them by surprise every time they opened a classroom door. So they sued a former tenant, Worsham College of Illinois, for trespass and creating a public nuisance. A mortuary science school, Worsham had been located in the school building for several years and left behind a number of skeletons, coffins and related funeral materials when they vacated the premises. Apparently the cache of mortuary memorabilia had wreaked havoc with school discipline.

A U.S. District court struck a blow for truth in celebrity endorsements when it ruled that the image of Woody Allen impersonator Phil Boroff had to carry a disclaimer that indicated that Boroff was not Allen. Allen had sued National Video, who had used Boroff in an advertising campaign. Allen claimed that the campaign implied that he endorsed the video rental company. In the settlement phase of the case, Allen was awarded $425,000. When asked if he really thought Boroff looked liked him, he replied, "It's hard for me to tell because I don't look at my face."

Mead Data Central, Inc. was also worried about consumer confusion. Mead sued the Toyota Motor Corporation for trademark infringement because they were concerned that the Lexus, Toyota's entry in the luxury car sweepstakes, might confuse individuals who used the Lexis legal research system developed by Mead Data. Mead attorney's argued that the confusion is made likely by the fact the research system contains information about automobiles.

Eddie Chatman was standing around, minding his own business, probably whistling "I'll Be There," when a pickup truck traveling at a fairly cautious 5 mph hit a pothole. The passenger door of the truck swung open and hit Chatman square in the back. He sued the truck driver and the unidentified city workers who, in his opinion, had failed to fulfill their municipal duties when they didn't fix that fateful pothole. A lower court tossed out the suit against the city workers on the grounds that they were protected by state liability laws.

But the New Jersey State Supreme Court disagreed, and in a 4-3 ruling said that public employees do have a duty to protect the public. More than that, Eddie could sue the individual workers who were supposed to fix that pothole but didn't. And he's going to.

Elmenia Lampley sued to have her two grown sons evicted from her home because they refused to get jobs, were sexually promiscuous, had foul mouths and smoked pot. The boys, 21 and 18, responded that they didn't smoke pot in the house but in the park. They answered their mother's charge that they were promiscuous with the comment, "Everyone has friends." Besides, they claimed their mom wasn't telling the whole story. They contend that the suit is based on the fact that their mom wants to get married and she doesn't want them in the way.

Picture the situation: April Genge is trying to buy $130 worth of Lotto tickets with numbers that she and her husband had selected. The clerk at the 7-Eleven only processes 12 sheets of numbers instead of 13. The line is getting longer. The clock is ticking. The clerk can't figure out which sheets were processed and which ones weren't. Customers are getting restless. That's when the assistant manager of the store handles the situation by giving Mrs. Genge $10 in computer-generated tickets and sends her on her way.

Well, April Genge is back, and she has her attorney with her. They claim that the clerk was negligent in handling the entries because they had the winning numbers on one of the sheets that didn't get processed. They would have won $20 million in the Lotto, but are willing to settle for $5 million.

The Cleveland Orchestra recorded Beethoven's Symphony No. 9 in 1961 under the direction of the late, great George Szell. Like much of the composer's later works, it had music you could hum but was kind of tough to dance to. Who would know that almost 30 years later, the Deaf One would meet the Gloved One? Certainly not the Cleveland Orchestra. It seems that Michael Jackson included 67 seconds worth of the orchestra's recording on his *Dangerous* album. It's heard at the beginning of "Will You be There?"

He should have called it "Will You Be There In Court?" because the orchestra sued Jackson for using it without their permission. MJJ Productions has agreed to credit the orchestra on all future releases. One big white glove for everybody.

As any casino veteran will tell you, if you want to play, you gotta pay. It seems that that concept eluded John W. Madsen. Mr. Madsen sued Boise State University on the grounds that they were discriminating against handicapped students by charging a fee for parking permits for handicapped spaces while there were free spaces available but at a distance from classrooms that made them inaccessible to the handicapped. Madsen lives on a fixed income and claimed that the fee prevented him from attending a class.

A federal appeals court said that while all that is very interesting, Madsen lacked the necessary standing to bring the suit because he had never applied for a parking permit. Case dismissed.

The Clinton administration has an added incentive to tackle health care reform. Last fall, Katherine Balog, a 60-year old unemployed accountant from Rancho Cucamonga, California, filed a suit against Bill Clinton and the Democratic Party. She claimed that Clinton's candidacy was causing her "serious emotional and mental stress." She sought reimbursement for medical treatment made necessary by stress caused by Clinton.

Perkins Coie, a high-profile law firm in Seattle and Los Angeles, billed Securities Environmental Systems (SES) a rather brisk $137,000 in fees for about 90 hours of legal work performed by Brian Saunders. SES took Perkins Coie to court because they think that a billable hour of $225 is a bit excessive, especially when you consider that Saunders wasn't an attorney. No law degree, no bar exam, no nothin' except for a resume that indicated that he probably should have been on the short list for Supreme Court nominations.

In their suit, SES claims that Perkins Coie is guilty of malpractice by not screening the resumes and employment history of their attorneys more carefully. Perkins Coie is standing by the billing rate. "All the work was supervised and approved by partners. We thought that Saunders did a good job on the account," said a company spokesman.

Ah, where to begin? The Maryland Attorney Grievance Commission thought that Attorney Stanley E. Protokowicz, Jr. should be disbarred. He fought his disbarment in the Maryland Court of Appeals where he admitted that he and a friend had consumed more than just a social beverage before breaking into the house of the friend's ex-wife. They were drunk and searching for stock certificates related to the friend's divorce case. That's when Protokowicz saw the family kitten, Max, and put him in the microwave for safekeeping. That's also when Protokowicz accidently started the microwave. You get the picture.

Protokowicz plead guilty to misdemeanor charges of breaking and entering and cruelty to animals, and got a 15-month suspended sentence. The court said that his actions were "a world apart from what the court, the profession and the public is entitled to expect from members of the bar." He was also ordered to get some treatment for his drinking. Luckily for Maryland residents, he can reapply for permission to practice law after one year.

Maybe ignorance isn't always bliss, but you would have a tough time proving that right now to Charles White, Jr. White and five other members of a local NAACP chapter sued the Buffalo Room restaurant for $200,000 in damages. The six claimed that they were refused service because they were black. A jury in Aikens, South Carolina awarded White $103,000, but said that he was the only one of the group that was entitled to damages because he was the only one of the group who didn't know that they were going to the Buffalo Room specifically to test its admission policy. Both the Buffalo Room and the other five plaintiffs are appealing the ruling.

It looks like Big Brother finally lost one. Chevron security officers ordered employee Garnet Overby to turn his pockets inside out as part of a random drug search. He refused and sued, arguing that the search constituted an invasion of his privacy. A jury agreed with Overby and ordered Chevron to turn their corporate pockets inside out and pay him $550,000 in damages. An 8-year employee of Chevron, Overby argued that he had fought in Vietnam to protect his constitutional right to be left alone. His attorneys made it clear that there was no probable cause or even a suspicion of drug use upon which to base the search.

Chevron had argued that they had a right to search Overby because he held a "safety-sensitive" position with the company. The jury awarded him $275,000 in actual damages and the rest for emotional distress.

The Oglala Sioux sued the Hornell Brewing Company, objecting to the name of Hornell's new product, Crazy Horse Malt Liquor. The name was selected to "celebrate our interest in the American West and the life and accomplishments of a great American warrior," according to Hornell chairman Don Vultaggio.

Attorney for the Sioux who sued, Bob Gough, argued, "People wouldn't stand for Martin Luther King Police Batons or Rodney King Police Batons." However, a federal court in New York didn't agree and ruled that Hornell's use of the name was protected by the First Amendment.

Black educator Russell Lawrence Lee said that he wanted to battle bigotry by taking the sting out of racially charged words. That's why he went into Ventura County Superior court to have his name legally change to "Misteri Nigger." The 'i' in "Misteri" would of course be silent, according to Lee. Neither the lower court or the appeals court thought that it was a good idea, and they denied his request and appeal.

In his decision, Justice Kenneth R. Yegan wrote, "We presume that at least some African-Americans would not be in agreement with the appellant's methods and might suffer embarrassment and shock by his use of the epithet as his official name." According to Yegan, Lee still has the common-law right to call himself anything he wants. The state, however, refuses to sanction it.

Former hostages Joseph Cicippio and David Jacobsen have sued Iran for $600 million on the grounds that the Iranian government sponsored "commercial terrorism." Jacobson explained that as hostages, they experienced poor health, depleted savings, a lack of job opportunities and had their careers destroyed. Both Jacobson, 61, and Cicippio, 62, are unemployed. Cicippio was the assistant comptroller of the American University in Beirut. Jacobsen was director of the University's hospital.

At last, a rock & roll copyright case that doesn't involve Michael Jackson or the Beatles. In 1969, Murray Wilson sold the rights to the songs of his Beach Boy son Brian to Irving Music for $700,000. The reclusive Brian finally emerged long enough to claim that the signature on the contract was a forgery and that he never relinquished the rights to his songs.

He sued Irving Music for $50 million. The financial terms of the eventual settlement have been kept secret, but it was estimated by original Beach Boy Mike Love that Wilson finally received $10 million for the songs. That's what Love states in the lawsuit he filed against Wilson. Love claims he deserves a piece of the settlement as a co-author of a number of the Beach Boys hits, including "Good Vibrations," which we can assume they won't be performing as a duet anytime in the near future.

If you are thinking of updating the Kama Sutra, you should read this first. A Los Angeles, California woman has sued her former lover (with the emphasis here on the word *former*) for $300,000, claiming that his rather spirited approach to making love was responsible for the broken bone in her neck. The former boyfriend is formally charged with battery and negligence by inflicting physical and emotional damage. The woman suffered a snapped disc in her neck and has experienced partial paralysis in her limbs. Her medical treatment has included spinal injections.

The defendant's attorney has argued that they didn't think that the assumption of risk applied to lovemaking since they were not engaged in S&M or any intentionally dangerous activity. The defendant has filed a claim under his homeowner's policy to cover his attorney's fees.

Judge Fred Staples sentenced Rodney Houf to 24 months in prison for unlawful delivery of cocaine, and then tacked on another 12 months to the sentence because he felt that Houf had lied during the trial. Houf didn't think that was fair, so he filed an appeal. The Washington Supreme Court reviewed his suit and agreed with him, ordering the county court to strike the extra year from his sentence.

Finding for the plaintiff, Justice Barbara Durham wrote, "Allowing an exceptional sentence based on the belief that the defendant lied at the trial would allow the defendant to be punished for a wholly unrelated crime with which he has never been charged, much less convicted."

"It's not easy being Zsa Zsa Gabor."

The state Supreme Court of Alabama made yet another cutting-edge legal ruling when they found that it is legal, according to state law, for individuals to be fired because of their gender. They were hearing the case of a disc jockey who was fired because she is a woman. Justice Hugh Maddox went out on a legal limb to explain the court didn't want to be misunderstood, they weren't condoning it, it's just that it's not illegal. Sure.

No question that they had the ashes to ashes part down. It was the next part that seemed to cause confusion at the Evergreen Memorial Park and Mausoleum in Riverside and the Mountain View Cemetery in San Bernadino, California. They were among seven facilities sued by San Diego attorney Robert Kilborne on behalf of approximately 70 clients. The suits claimed that the facilities had co-mingled the remains of a number of individuals, as well as committing a host of other procedural improprieties. Five of the suits were settled prior to trial.

Maybe it was show and tell day. Who knows? Anyway, Phillip J. Fielding, a ninth-grader in Kelso, Washington thought it was a good idea to bring a firearm to school. The school authorities didn't think it was a good idea, or appropriate even by today's standards, so they expelled him. His parents didn't think that was very fair, what with Phil being a good student and all, so they filed a suit contending that Philip had been denied due process because the school had failed to try other forms of punishment before expelling him. They filed the suit after a judge rejected their request for a restraining order to block the expulsion. The NRA has yet to issue a comment.

Those G.I. Joe guys are back in court again. This time the Federal Trade Commission charged that the ad for Hasbro's G.I. Joe Battle Copter falsely claimed that the toy helicopter could fly. Hasbro agreed to pay a $175,000 settlement. The FTC wanted to make sure that the public knew that the Battle Copter could not actually "hover and fly in a sustained and directed manner" as depicted in the ad, and that the toy had been suspended by wires in the commercial.

Next thing you know they'll be telling us it doesn't fire real rockets.

Cleveland authorities indicted Jeffrey Mann, 36, on murder charges claiming that he had ordered his pet pit bull to attack his common-law wife, Angela. The pit bull was being kept at an animal shelter as evidence until the trial. The D.A.'s office claims that this is the first time they have ever heard of someone using a pit bull as a murder weapon.

Cynthia Albritton used to go by the moniker of Cynthia Plaster Caster. That was back in the late 60's and early 70's, when her primary source of amusement was making plaster casts of the... ah... instruments of various pop musicians. She had asked a fellow by the name of Herbert L. Cohen to store 25 of them in his home. Cohen, for whatever reason, asked for and received Ms. Albritton's permission in 1971 to make some silver and bronze copies of the plaster originals. When she asked for the return of the originals in 1988, Cohen told her that the originals no longer existed.

In fact, Cohen claimed ownership of the copies,

contending that Albritton was really working for Bizarre Productions, a company of which he was part owner, back when she was casting the very intimate likenesses of folks like Jimi Hendrix, Eddie Brigati of the Rascals and Anthony Newley. That's when Ms. Albritton did the very un-60's thing of suing Cohen for the return of the copies. Finding for the plaintiff, Judge Lillian M. Stevens wrote, "Any reproductions are the progeny of the original casts and title did not pass to anyone." The casts were then released to Albritton. Anthony Newley?

In a criminal action in North Carolina, a jury convicted televangelist Rev. Jim Whittington of defrauding a Florida widow of $900,000 in cash and property. In his own defense, Whittington said that he thought that things would have been different if he was anything other than a televangelist. Could be. But if he thinks that a new profession would change his luck, the widow might want to consider changing her name for the same reason. Valeria Lust has to be a heavy load to carry.

In other crime fighting news, Los Angeles, California City Attorney James Hahn filed a civil suit against the Blythe Street gang of Van Nuys. The suit defines the gang as an unincorporated association of approximately 350 members. In addition to a curfew, the suit seeks a number of controls on gang members: no clothing that identifies them as gang members, no weapons, no devices that can be used in drug trafficking (such as beepers or walkie-talkies), no marking pens, no burglary tools, no loitering and no entering private property without permission. Best of all, the suit would prohibit them from "Doing any repairs or maintenance to cars on the street that do not belong to the person doing the work." That's good.

The city of Chicago publicly blamed the Great Lakes Dredge & Dock Co. for starting the flood that caused more than $1 billion in damages to downtown businesses in 1991. Not wanting to take the rap for the biggest thing to hit Chicago since the Great Fire of 1871, Great Lakes said not hardly and sued the city, claiming that not only didn't they start the flood, they were never told about the 50-mile system of freight tunnels located under the city. Oops!

Homer Hardy's wife died of a heart attack the same day that tickets for a concert by country music star Garth Brooks went on sale. You may not see the immediate connection, but Hardy, a Tulsa, Okalahoma physician, did and sued Southwestern Bell for $35 million. Hardy claimed that his repeated attempts to reach emergency services by dialing 911 were met with a busy signal. He also contends in his suit that

Southwestern Bell was negligent when it failed to take adequate precautions to avoid having their circuits swamped by fans trying to purchase concert tickets over the phone.

Brooks was not named in the suit.

Raymond Ternes is the president of a group of individuals who allege that they have been cheated in divorce settlements. Ternes contended that many judges have ignored the plight of the members of their group. Not anymore. Ternes went to court and placed liens against the homes of seven court commissioners and judges in the state of Washington as a means of getting their attention. While it is illegal to place a fraudulent lien, the lien does serve to cloud the title to the houses and must be removed before the house can be sold, which can be a very cumbersome process. The local DA has indicated that Ternes may face criminal charges if he continues to 'lien' on the judges.

Perhaps it was Voltaire who said it best when he observed that if Zsa Zsa Gabor did not exist, man would have been compelled to invent her. Or as she put it herself recently, "I have to look like Zsa Zsa Gabor and it's not easy being Zsa Zsa Gabor." Ms. Gabor was testifying in a breach-of-contract law suit brought against her by Leonard Safir, president of Hollywood Fantasy Corp. of San Antonio Texas. Safir claimed that he hired Gabor to mix and mingle with guests at a "Hollywood star camp" and participate in short video productions with them.

According to Safir, she ruined his business when she refused to appear at the event. Gabor said that the agreement that they had really wasn't a contract and even if it was a contract, Safir failed to produce the makeup, hairdressers and support systems that let Zsa Zsa be Zsa Zsa. The jury found for Safir, but the case is under appeal.

Even millionaires can have a rough year now and then. Take Joaquin de Monet, for instance. First his Napa Valley mansion blows up . Then he sues his wife for divorce, alleging that she seduced his 15-year old son from a previous marriage. Mrs. Monet's attorneys countered with a request to dismiss the suit, claiming that this kind of family conflict doesn't belong in the courts. How about on TV?

We all know it takes money to make money, but this is ridiculous. The state of Connecticut sued the Trevor B. Ewing Memorial Foundation for allegedly channeling funds raised for brain tumor research to a number of other pursuits including: polo matches (2), flowers, photography services and $648 to fly the Queen's hat maker to Connecticut to judge a women's hat contest. The state contends that the foundation raised approximately $155,195 between 1990 and 1992 but directed only a total of $5,000 to research. The overhead must be killin' 'em.

Elizabeth and Patrick Meegan had been married for 23 years before divorcing in May of 1988. Patrick had a sizeable disposable income and was directed by the court to pay Elizabeth $739 in monthly support payments. In 1991 Mr. Meegan decided that he could hear the Lord calling and he resigned his successful sales position to enter a religious community in Arizona. That's when the support checks stopped. Elizabeth Meegan went to court to sue for continuation of support, but the Santa Ana District Court didn't see it her way.

Justice Henry Moore ruled that, even though he was living off of investments and approximately $90,000 in savings, Mr. Meegan's income had been reduced to zero, and he was no longer obligated to make the monthly support payments. The ruling also implied that the support payments were not Elizabeth Meegan's sole source of income. Patrick Meegan said that he planned to stay with the religious order in Arizona for at least five years, and that he hoped to become a priest. Justice Henry said that he believes him. Go in peace, everybody.

n 1990, both *USA Today* and *The Star* ran surveys using "900" telephone numbers that made it possible for readers to vote for the hottest member of the singing group, The New Kids On the Block. Now, a wise guy might say the answer was none of them, since the papers only took in $1,900 in revenues. But that didn't stop the Kids from suing both papers, claiming that the contest violated their exclusive right to use the group name. They also charged that the papers engaged in false advertising and unfair competition.

The 9th Circuit Court didn't see it that way. They ruled that extending the group's trademark to newspaper articles and polls would also make advertising impossible. As to the argument that the use of the 900 number directed money away from promotions run by the group, Judge Alex Kosinski said that the group's trademark did not allow them "to control their fan's use of their own money." The court issued a 3-0 decision against the Kids, as has many a music critic over the years.

Although it sounded like a script for a Sci-Fi movie, the suit of *People v. Defendant X* described a situation that took the concept of plea bargaining to a whole new level. In a Los Angeles, California appeal suit, Defendant X described a "binding contract" in which he agreed to set up at least two felony drug buys for the law enforcement in return for five years probation on a guilty plea. If he failed to "complete the agreed-upon contract," he would be sentenced to eight

131

years in state prison. After what he called a good faith effort to "complete the contract," he failed to set up the drug buys and asked the court to withdraw his guilty plea. The judge refused on the grounds that he had entered into a binding contract.

The appeal court found for Defendant X, ruling that " to give a negotiated plea the form and function of a civil complaint" is inconsistent with the role of the judiciary.

Research and authenticity are one thing, but Capt. John Orr of the Glendale Fire Department may have taken them one step too far. Orr, who has written a novel about a firefighter who is a pyromaniac, was convicted on three counts of arson. The Fresno, California jury ruled that Orr set the fires while attending an arson investigators conference.

Sadu Singh Johl is a Sikh and, as such, he is required by his religion to wear a turban. He is also a mo-ped rider and, as such, he is required by California law to wear a helmet. As anyone who has tried to get a helmet on over a turban will tell you, the two are mutually exclusive. Johl saw the conflict as a matter of religious freedom and took the matter to court, appealing his $54 traffic fine for riding without a helmet. Court Commissioner Michael Lewis thought that Johl's suit was without merit, explaining that Johl was free to take other forms of public transportation, such as buses and trains, that allowed him to wear his turban. "Let us go to the highest court," said Johl. "We are right." As you can see, this one could go on forever.

Our Unctuous Spawn of Privilege Award goes to the teenage daughter of a millionaire Orange County, California businessman. The businessman agreed to pay his daughter a monthly allowance of $2,000, American, to keep her in tube tops and tanning lotion. He even agreed to increase it by a "reasonable" amount when the net worth of his business jumped by a cool $20 mill. That's when his ex-wife, herself a millionaire, jumped in and said no, "Muffin" needs at least $15 large (as in thousand) a month just for the basics: $3,333 for life insurance, $2,000 for clothing and $2,000 for credit cards. You know, the basics. So she took her ex-husband to court to increase his monthly contribution.

Well, the court got out their calculators and said no, it's only $9,000 a month that's needed by the typical Orange County Teenager, or judicial muttering to that effect, and ruled that Dad now, by law, has to kick in $6,000 samolians, as in greenbacks, as in buckolas a month to prevent "Muffin" from becoming the Poor Little Match Girl. They based their ruling on the Civil Code, which states that a parent's first obligation is to support his or her children according to the parent's circumstances. The common sense (i.e.: minority) position was voiced by Judge David Sills, who said that just because her mom wants her daughter to be a "power shopper," law does not require her dad to pay for it. Kind of makes you want to take a shower, doesn't it?

All you folks who have your garden tools and compact discs out on loan, take note. There is a family in court in Connecticut over what constitutes a gift and what constitutes an extended loan. Ann Rylands claims that she received a violin, an authentic Guadagnini worth $200,000, from her father in 1963 as a gift and has used that violin professionally as a concert violinist. When she entered a treatment center last year she asked her mother to care for the violin and her mother agreed. Now her mom won't give it back. In fact, her mom and her sister are claiming in court that the violin was never a gift, but rather a loan -- an extended loan of a $200,000 violin for approximately 30 years. Yeah, happens all the time.

For Wayne and Judie Johnson it all comes down to life, liberty and the pursuit of the Chicago Bears football team. The city of Pleasanton, California has an ordinance that places a 10-foot height limit on satellite antennas. The Johnsons claim that they need a 14-foot antenna, minimum, to pull in the Bears games on their satellite dish and sued the city twice on the grounds that the ordinance violated their rights under the First and Fourteenth Amendments.

The 9th Circuit court cut to the core of the argument when they ruled for the city, finding that the problem was not that the Johnsons needed a 14-foot antenna, but that the best place on their property for the antenna was already occupied by a swimming pool. If they could place an antenna on the sight of the pool, they could get adequate reception with an antenna that complied with the ordinance. In the words of the court, "The case becomes as much a freedom to swim case as a freedom of speech case." They also suggested that the Johnsons should get cable.

Matthew D. was 16 and a ward of the court. He was on probation for striking another student in a manner that broke the student's jaw and teeth. Matthew D. was also a practicing Satanist, and prohibited by the terms of his probation from associating with other Satanists. And, as you might have guessed, according to the suit brought by Matthew's court-appointed attorney, this is not just another case of a heavy metal delinquent who needs his attitude adjusted. Not by a long shot. According to the suit, Matthew's constitutional right to worship Satan in the fellowship of other practicing Satanists has been violated by the terms.

The appeals court where the suit was heard didn't think so, ruling that "violence is inherent in Satan worship" and that the restrictions furthered the court's intention of rehabilitating Matthew. Though Matthew remained on probation, the court affirmed that he was free to continue to go do that voodoo that he did so well.

An appeals court in the state of Washington has ruled that there really is a difference between a sling shot and a slung shot. Enough of a difference to throw out the conviction of a 13-year old boy who was inappropriately charged with using a slung shot to knock out windows in a house. It seems that when a prosecutor was filling out the forms to charge the boy, he saw the term "slung shot" and assumed that it was either a misspelling or was the same weapon. Well, we all know what happens when we assume, don't we?

It turns out that a slung shot is similar to what David used on Goliath, and not what the 13-year old used on the windows. And that was enough of a reason for the appeals court to let the little alleged vandal go free.

The Stephen Foster Liberation Front can rest easy tonight. An appeals court has ruled that a "black face" skit performed by the brothers at Sigma Chi fraternity at George Mason University was protected by the First Amendment. The fraternity sued when university officials attempted to take disciplinary action against them for the song and dance performance parodying blacks. The skit took place at a fundraising event.

Calling the skit an "exercise of teenage campus excess," Judge James M. Sprouse said that "the low quality of entertainment does not necessarily weigh in the First Amendment." OK everybody, "My Old Kentucky Home" on one.

L et's start with your basic unemployed stripper, the lovely and vivacious Bonnie Lynn Bradigan, whose suit for fraud was dismissed because she missed the filing deadline by two months. She was suing to prevent her boyfriend, the son of a well-known Southern California newscaster, from using a timely bankruptcy filing to get out of paying Bradigan $150,000 he owed from a judgment she had filed against him at an earlier date. Sounds like prom night at Piranha High.

Anyway, hell hath no fury like an "artiste" scorned, so when the fraud suit was dismissed, Bradigan began to leave threatening messages on the phone machine of the judge who dismissed the case. Things like "I've got friends...who won't let you hurt me...friends, they're not going to like it. They'll probably shoot me when I get my money, who else knows, who else might be shot or murdered." And, "I got screwed out of $150,000 so far. I'm real angry and I'm not responsible for what I do any more because I'm not myself." Well, the court thought she was enough herself to convict her of threatening to assault a federal bankruptcy judge.

Steven Barton sued his attorney, Earl Rick Stokes, for malpractice. Barton contends that one night while they were away for the weekend, Stokes introduced himself to Barton "in the Biblical sense" while Barton slept. According to the suit, Stokes constantly cajoled Barton to have sex with him in lieu of billing him for legal services and just generally drove him nuts until he agreed to settle a suit that Barton now believes he should have won. He sued Stokes for approximately $44,000. Stokes and his former law partners filed a cross complaint for $10,730 to obtain unpaid attorney's fees.

The jury eventually found for Barton, which might indicate that in the 90s there really is more than one way for your attorney to do you.

Jerry W. May was a brickmason's tender by trade. That was before he fell from a 9-foot high scaffold and sustained injuries that left him unable to return to the job. Jerry saw Sam Spital's advertising on television and retained him as his attorney. Mr. Spital has been described as the third-largest attorney advertiser in the country. As an attorney, Mr. May found Mr. Spital to be an effective television personality and little else. Through Mr. Spital's efforts, May only received $2,000 in compensation for what he considered to be a career-ending injury.

So he sued Spital for $3.9 million. The jury only awarded May a paltry $2.5 million which included $2.05 million in false advertising and mishandling the May case, and $506,000 which the jury reasoned May deserved from the original case. It would appear from the size of the jury's award that the earning potential of brickmason's tenders had grown significantly during the Reagan years. Mr. May later indicated that the verdict against Spital had changed his belief in the judicial system. He did not indicate whether or not his belief in television advertising had changed, as well.

A Los Angeles appeals court performed a Herculean task of sorting legal apples and oranges when it ruled on the appeal filed by the family of a man who was shot by the Los Angeles, California police. Yes, the officers who were charged in the shooting should be retried, despite the fact that the first verdict favored them. And no, even though Judge A. Andrew Hauck had engaged in "some injudicious behavior," he had not disqualified himself from presiding over a retrial of the case. This is despite the fact that he referred to the attorneys for the family as "boobs" and jailed attorney Robert Cook during the course of the first trial.

The Sun assumed that Nellie Mitchell was dead. That's why the tabloid ran her photo with a caption that proclaimed her to be a 101-year-old letter carrier from Australia who had quit her job because she was pregnant. Ms. Mitchell didn't care for that characterization, and sued the Sun. She was awarded $1.5 million in punitive and compensatory damages. This was later reduced to $850,000 in punitive damages. In reality, Ms. Mitchell is not 101, but a sprightly 96.

"When you're running full speed, you can't really stop and say 'Oh, that's a girl.'"

Two passengers were killed when the car Jeffrey Smith of Michgan was driving pulled into the passing lane and collided head-on with an oncoming car. Charged with negligent homocide in criminal court, Smith contended that he shouldn't be held responsible for the deaths because neither of the victims had been wearing his safety belt as required by state law. In his attorney's words, "Death would not have resulted had the victims been following the law."

The jury agreed.

The woman who has forged a career out of turning oversize letters in public while wearing an evening gown, yes *that* Vanna White, has sued Samsung. She claims that the consumer electronics giant used a robot in one of its commercials, and that the robot bore a striking resemblance to her. This made Ms. White very uncomfortable on the personal level, and perhaps a little nervous on the professional level, as well.

The U.S. Supreme Court ruled that the commercial was not, as Samsung's lawyers argued, a parody, meaning Vanna had the right to sue if she was concerned that the public might confuse the robot and her.

Whoever has been promoting the notion of the global village forgot to tell Roy Staublein. Rene Vasquez and Rodrigo Ochoa claimed that Staublein approached them while they were enjoying a cold one in his tavern, and told them that they would have to leave if they continued to speak to one another in Spanish. They also claimed that he called the police when they protested his announcement.

Vasquez and Ochoa sued Staublein, claiming unspecified damages and arguing that he discriminated against them because of their "ancestry or ethnic characteristics." Staublein said he didn't do it.

While sitting on death row in Walla Walla, Washington, triple murderer Charles Coughlin Campbell began to meditate on the method and nature of his ever-approaching execution. He eventually came to be of the opinion that hanging, his in particular, violated the Eighth Amendment's provision against cruel and unusual punishment. So he took his case to the Supreme Court. His attorney argued that hanging carried an "unavoidable and unacceptable risk of decapitation or slow strangulation." Condemned men in the state of Washington get to choose between hanging and lethal injection. Those who refuse to choose, such as Campbell, are hung.

U.S. District Court judge John Coughenour dismissed the claim, stating that "the pain necessarily involved in the extinguishment of life" did not violate the Constitution. This one is on its way to the court of appeals.

Joyce Welp and Michael Bachman took their late English sheepdog and canine companion of ten years, Ruffian, to be buried at the Long Island Pet Cemetery. They dished out $1083 for a headstone, the burial and the understanding that Ruffian got to take his pink blanket, his toys and his collar with him to that big water bowl in the sky. The folks at the cemetery said no problem.

Welp and Bachman began to worry when they saw that in June of 1991, the owners of the cemetery had been charged with mail fraud for holding mass cremations and burying as many as 250,000 pets in common graves. Welp and Bachman opened Ruffian's grave, only to find neither the pink blanket, nor (you guessed it) the deceased. The experience sent them both into psychotherapy, then into the courtroom. Of the

$10 million they asked for, the court awarded $1.2 million.

❽

L ife's a bitch, and then you change your sex. But that's not the end of it, as Jacqueline Farell found out. Farell, a transsexual inmate at the Los Angeles county jail, was forced to move from the women's jail to the men's facility. Her $5 million federal lawsuit against the County of Los Angeles, its sheriff and various public officials alleges that, since moving to the men's clubhouse, she has been harassed both by inmates and sheriff's deputies, thus violating her constitutional rights.

❽

H e's back, the guy you want on your corner if you live on a cul de sac, an attorney for all seasons, Sam Spital. Spital was sued by yet another former client for "legal malpractice, fraud, deceit, negligent representation, intentional infliction of emotional distress and libel and slander." It seems that Spital's staff missed by one day the one-year deadline for filing the client's personal injury suit against Bic, manufacturers of the disposable and occasionally explodable cigarette lighters. She was injured on February 1, 1989, and Spital's crack staff filed the lawsuit on February 2, 1990. This, despite several assurances by Spital that the case was moving along nicely.

The former client's lawsuit argued that the now-legendary television commercials for Spital's law firm "imply that Spital will personally be involved in and oversee each case." In depositions prior to the trial, Spital stated that he never personally tried a product liability suit and that he was not able to name a single instance in which he had actually represented anyone in any kind of lawsuit. Spital's defense included arguments that 1989 was actually a leap year, and that his former client was incompetent to sue him because court documents prepared for her in her case against Bic showed that she admitted she was "insane at the time of the accident."

❽

A black Washington, D.C. woman charged Kinko's copy center with racial discrimination, asking for $4 million for emotional distress because two employees at the Capitol Hill branch wouldn't let her use the copier and the stapler.

The two employees also were black. Case dismissed.

❽

Madeline Crawley, 19, of Sacramento, California, has sued St. Mary's College, claiming that the school's director of intramural sports was negligent when he failed to tell male players in the school's flag football league that they should use less force against the female players.

In her lawsuit, Crawley seeks damages for

injuries she described as "serious," when she was allegedly struck full force in the chest and shoulders during a game by Berkley philosophy major, Paul Karst. With Cartesian economy, Karst responded, "When you're running full speed you can't really stop and say, 'Oh, that's a girl.'"

Janice Goodman claimed that she developed a repetitive stress injury while working for the Boeing Company, where her job was to press a button thousands of times a day in order to photograph documents at the Boeing plant south of Seattle, Washington. In order to ease the pain caused by the repetitive motion, she eventually had to wear a splint on each hand. She sued Boeing, but a jury found the company not to be liable. They did award Goodman $1.6 million, however, because she was able to prove that, despite her pain, her supervisor demanded that she work faster, and kept her on the camera longer than anyone else.

In an effort to justify the award, Goodman's attorney said, "Her boss sneered at her. He called her stupid and made fun of her braces."

8

Proving the adage that some folks look mighty different the next morning than they did the night before, a Tufts University sophomore has charged a Colby College football player with sexual assault. It seems that, following a football game between the two schools, a fraternity party ensued, during which the coed went to bed with a fellow Tufts fellow. The trouble arose, however, when she woke up, only to find next to her the defendant, who had remained silent as could be as she administered oral sex to the man she thought to be Bachelor Number One.

The judicial board at Colby College has recommended acquittal for the football player.

⑧

An inebriated New York City man lost his arm when he fell onto the tracks and into the path of an oncoming subway train. Naturally, he sought damages from the city's transit authority. A jury decided that not only was the incident not his fault, but also that a subway worker should have recognized that he was drunk and ushered him from the platform. The award? $9.3 milllion. That's a lot of tokens.

Fortunately for the champions of common sense, a judge reversed the decision, stating that the "jury acted irrationally."

⑧

Philadelphia real estate manager, Robert Kropinski, spent 11 years seeking the "perfect state of life" promised by Transcendental Meditation groups founded by part time media star, guru Maharishi Mahesh Yogi, for whom he was a student and teacher. The result? Pyschological disorders, of course. In a decision by a U.S. district-court jury in Washington, D.C. that left a spokesman for the organizations "surprised and puzzled," Kropinski was awarded nearly $138,000 in damages.

One of the promises that Kropinski claimed went unfulfilled was that he had been told he would, through self-levitation, be taught to "fly," but he only learned how to "hop with the legs folded in the lotus position."

I n yet another case surrounding Stephen King and his novel, *Misery*, a woman sued him along with seven government officials, including Senator William Cohen of Maine, then vice chairman of the Senate Intelligence Committee; Howell Heflin, chairman of the Senate Ethics Committee; Senate Majority Leader George Mitchell; Speaker of the House Tom Foley; and Brent Scowcroft, National Security Advisor. According to the woman, the defendants "Placed illegal electronic surveillance on [her] for transmission of her Person on a continuous basis...to act as the 'Living Character' of Stephen King's pulp novel *Misery*, violating the Fifth Amendment of the United States Constitution's guarantee of due process of law."

She alleged that the story came from her head, therefore rendering King's authorship of the book in violation of federal copyright law. An assistant U.S. attorney submitted a lengthy brief, the bottom line of which asks for $25 million in damages. The complaint, however, did not indicate from whom those damages were sought.

American-born Randolf Fritz, in prison in Oregon, renounced his U.S. citizenship in a 1990 lawsuit against, among others, then Attorney General Dick Thornburgh, the Immigration and Naturalization Service and the Oregon State Department of Corrections. Because he had no green card, Fritz contended, he couldn't do his prison work, and was a deportable alien who should exit at once the land of his birth.

Fritz claimed that, as he was no longer an American, he has become a "vassal," a point which he supported in a document titled "A Manifesto of Vassalage." In an excerpt from that modern classic, he wrote, "I do absolutely repudiate all allegiance, fidelity, fealty and oaths of any prince, potentate, state sovereignty, suzerainty, person, sociostructure, enterprise, and international organization to whom or which I have heretofore been a subject, citizen, member party, covantee or covanteer."

Returning home to Rochester, New York from a trip to Ft. Myers, Florida, the Feinstock family were puzzled to find their arthritic, blind and deaf dog, Ari, missing from the plane's luggage. They found, later, that Ari had been taken off the plane in Tampa and left circling endlessly on an airport conveyor belt. So the family sued USAir in the dog's name.

The Feinstocks determined that Ari's trauma was worth $50,000, but U.S. District Judge Michael Telesca begged (so to speak) to differ, stating that Ari is not a citizen of the United States, and therefore not qualified to sue. Ari was eventually returned to the safety of its family, traumitized and penniless.

❽

Federal drug agents were so impressed by Andrew Sokolow's black jumpsuit and array of sparkling jewlery as he arrived in Honolulu Airport from Miami, that they obtained a search warrant. When they opened his bag, they found a mere 1000 grams of cocaine, as in one kilo, as in 2.2 pounds, as in felony offense.

Sokolow pleaded that there was no reasonable cause for search, with which a federal appeals court agreed, stating that "style of clothing...is an extremely unreliable ground" for suspicion of a crime. It reasoned that someone might equally be suspected of insider trading simply because he "wears a pinstriped suit and a gold Cartier watch."

❽

What began as a schoolboy's dream ended up as a parents' nightmare. Philip Sciarra, 6, of Bridgehampton, New York, was not being assigned homework by his first-grade teacher at the Hampton Day School. That suited little Philip fine, but his parents felt there was a need for such homework, and proceeded to sue the school for $1500 for breach of contract. The sum was to cover time spent tutoring Philip at home.

An attorney for Hampton responded, "The school afforded the boy his full educational opportunities." The jury in the case agreed, and the case was rejected, with the provision that the Sciarras cough up the $975 tuition they had withheld from the school.

❽

In case you're wondering why the words *noon* and *midnight* exist, a New Jersey superior court may have provided a clue. In a case presented to the court, Dennis Hart had received a ticket for parking in Wildwood at a prohibited hour. The ticket was issued at 1:30pm on a street where a sign declared that parking was not permitted from "8am to 12pm." Hart argued that 12pm meant noon, while the city maintained that the restriction clearly meant midnight.

In the legal equivalent of baseball's 'tie goes to the runner,' Hart's attorney, Louis Hornstine, argued, "If there is an ambiguity in a statute, the court rules in favor of the defendant."

❽

Lori Colin began to get nervous when her husband, Jack Lee Colin, began waving guns around at home. She remembered that when the two first met at a party, Jack had told her that his parents had been killed in a car accident years earlier. When she began to do a little sleuthing on her own, however, she found that Jack had actually shot the couple to death himself, but had been cleared of homocide charges by reason of insanity. So she sued him.

In response to her demand for a divorce and $20,000 for "emotional distress," Jack's attorney countered that Jack was in no way legally obliged to reveal the...um...skeletons in his closet. A nominal out-of-court settlement was arranged.

❽

Professional psychic Judith Haimes underwent a CAT scan at Temple University Hospital as part of her treatment for a brain tumor. Haimes sued the hospital after experiencing an allergic reaction to the dye used in the scan that she claimed made her feel as if her head was going to explode.

Despite being ordered by the judge to ignore the psychic damage claims, the jury returned after deliberating only 45 minutes with an award of $986,000. Makes you wonder if Haimes used her powers to help pick the jury.

❽

There is more news on the pig front. This time the dateline is Guilford, Connecticut, where the city fathers and mothers have sued Deborah Gallagher for $9,000 over a bit of real, live pre-cured bacon that she calls Dolly. After several warnings, Gallagher was arrested for failing to remove Dolly from her property. The town contended that the pig's proximity to a day care center created a health hazard.

Gallagher finally removed Dolly and the charges

were dropped, but that wasn't good enough for the officials of this "greene country towne." Estimating that they had already dropped a cool $15,000 in their legal battle over Dolly's removal, the town launched their $90,000 punitive salvo across Gallagher's bow.

❽

Too bad Charles Johnson couldn't find a way to use his own invention. Johnson claimed to have invented "The Club," a device designed to prevent car theft. Johnson also claimed that the device was stolen from him by Winner International, the company that now manufactures the product.

Winner International has agreed to an out-of-court settlement in excess of $10 million.

❽

In 1984, Lee Grant was the top salesman at Darby Buick in Sarasota, Florida. One year later, he was let go. Grant, 62, thought that he was a victim of age discrimination and filed an appropriate law suit. Darby Buick replied that it wasn't a suit that was at issue. It was more like a sport coat. Grant's multicolored one in particular. And they weren't too crazy about his fuchsia one, either.

In fact, Grant's former employers were quick to point out that his dismissal came on the heels of a memo that urged all salesman to begin dressing in a way that improved the image of the dealership. Grant didn't see anything wrong with his fashion selections.

153

He defended his multicolored sportcoat as a rainbow plaid that actually went with all of his trousers.

⑧

A quick "Hey babe" and a tug of a pony tail set a Colorado Springs obstetrician back $65,000. Nurse Jean Kovel sued her boss, Dr. William Emeis, saying that his greeting caused her to suffer excruciating pain in her neck, back and shoulder and that she had to hire a maid to help with the household chores. During the pretrial investigation, Dr. Emeis said that he couldn't remember the incident. Bet he won't forget it now.

⑧

Some pantyhose are more slippery than others. That's a fact of life, at least according to Myrna Golden of Chicago, Illinois. Ms. Golden slipped, broke her ankle and claimed that it was the "unusually" slippery nature of the pantyhose made by Pennaco Hoisery, Inc. that caused her injury. However, neither a lower court nor the appeals court thought that she had a legal leg to stand on. Both dismissed the suit.

⑧

The admonition "as you sow, so shall ye reap" finally caught up with Lueking family of Nebraska. In a U. S. district court they were directed to pay the federal government $1 million in a civil suit as part of a

$2.52 million settlement. The Luekings had been sub-dividing a single farm among 15 family members in order to get multiple subsidy payments of $50,000 each from the feds. In the interest of efficiency, the Luekings decided that it would be a lot easier just to subdivide the farm on paper without really breaking it up. The federal government didn't agree. It was the largest settlement of its kind against a single farmer.

⑧

N egligent, unreasonable and uncontrolled dancing" was the basis of the law suit that Dave McGregor filed against his former square-dance partner, Connie Coston. McGregor contends that Coston broke his left leg when she executed a wild kick while they were dancing the Evansville Indiana Freedom Festival.

According to McGregor, Ms. Coston was dancing in a "way not called for." Break dancing, perhaps?

⑧

S eventy-four-year old Adeline Miller was minding her own business as she returned to Minnesota from Las Vegas via Air California. That's when the crew of the plane allowed another passenger, one Larry White, to take the microphone so he could congratulate a friend on his good luck in Vegas. White launched into an impromptu lounge act that included a warning that the plane was about to crash. Miller didn't think that it was so funny. In fact, she said in her suit for $300,000 worth of damages that the monologue caused her to have chest pains, claustrophobia, a fear of snowbanks, riding in cars and, of course, flying.

A jury agreed with her, sort of. They awarded her $10,000 and $226 in medical expenses. The jury then distributed the degree of negligence in the following manner: Air California- 80%, Larry White-19% and Adeline Miller-1%. That's what you get for believing a bad lounge act.

In a suit that many of us would like to file, particularly on a Monday morning, a man recently submitted a handwritten, one-page complaint in U.S. District Court in Washington, D.C. in which he sued the Supreme Court and The World.

His basis for the complaint was that the world was against him.

Sources

Philadelphia Inquirer
Philadelphia Daily News
New York Post
New York Daily News
Washington Post
AP Wire Service
Los Angeles Daily Journal
Los Angeles Times
Student Lawyer Magazine
Rapid City Journal
Sioux Falls Journal
ABA Journal
Wall Street Journal
Newsweek
Insight Magazine
Nolo News
San Francisco Examiner

Newark Star Ledger
Cincinnati Post
Playboy
USA Today
West Palm Beach Post
Miami Herald
Louisville Courier Journal
St. Paul Pioneer Press-Dispatch
Arizona Republic
Denver Post
Asbury Park Press
Dallas Morning News
Courier News
Time
Omaha World Herald
Milwaukee Journal
Salt Lake Tribune
Orlando Sentinel
Atlanta Journal Constitution
Harper's Magazine
The Tennessean
U.S. News and World Report
The Litigation Explosion, Dutton Press 1991
Supreme Folly, W.W. Norton 1990